# The New Management
of Local Government

INSTITUTE OF LOCAL GOVERNMENT STUDIES

*Approaches in Public Policy*
Edited by Steve Leach and John Stewart

*Local Government: The Conditions of Local Choice*
John Stewart

*Between Centre and Locality*
*The Politics of Public Policy*
Edited by Stewart Ranson, George Jones and Kieron Walsh

*The Changing Government of Education*
Edited by Stewart Ranson and John Tomlinson

# The
# New Management
# of Local
# Government

JOHN STEWART

*Institute of Local Government Studies*
*University of Birmingham*

For the
Institute of Local Government Studies
University of Birmingham

ALLEN & UNWIN
London     Boston     Sydney

**Allen & Unwin (Publishers) Ltd,**
**40 Museum Street, London WC1A 1LU, UK**

Allen & Unwin (Publishers) Ltd,
Park Lane, Hemel Hempstead, Herts HP2 4TE, UK

Allen & Unwin, Inc.,
8 Winchester Place, Winchester, Mass. 01890, USA

Allen & Unwin (Australia) Ltd,
8 Napier Street, North Sydney, NSW 2060, Australia

First published in 1986

---

**British Library Cataloguing in Publication Data**

Stewart, John, *1929 Mar. 19–*
    The new management of local government.
    1. Local government – Great Britain
    I. Title   II. University of Birmingham, *Institute of*
    *Local Government Studies* 352.041 JS 3158
    ISBN 0–04–352232–7
    ISBN 0–04–352233–5 Pbk

---

**Library of Congress Cataloging in Publication Data**

Stewart, John David, 1929–
    The new management of local government.
    Bibliography: p.
    Includes index.
    1. Local government – Great Britain.   I. Title
    JS3158.S87   1986   352.041   86–10950
    ISBN 0-04-352232-7 (alk. paper)
    ISBN 0-04-352233-5 (pbk.: alk. paper)

---

Set in 10 on 11 point Sabon by Computape (Pickering) Ltd.
and printed in Great Britain by
Billing and Son Ltd, London and Worcester

# Contents

# Preface

This book is based on my work at the Institute of Local Government Studies over many years. It draws especially upon my work for the Local Government Training Board, which has commissioned me to report on the changing management of local government and on whose behalf I have visited nearly one hundred authorities in recent years. There are many to thank:

- the councillors and officers in local authorities, upon whose ideas and experience I have drawn;
- the authorities who have allowed me time and space for interviews and discussions and whose reports I have used or quoted in this book;
- my colleagues at the Institute and the many discussions that have stimulated ideas and thoughts;
- the staff of the Local Government Training Board where the discussions are different and challenge in their difference, providing a new stimulus;
- the Local Government Training Board both for the support for my work which has been invaluable and for permission to draw upon the reports I have prepared for them;
- the secretarial staff at the Institute for their continuous help;
- Mrs Sheila Minton for her work in typing up the manuscript of this book.

Specifically I want to thank Steve Leach, Stewart Ransom and Kieron Walsh from the Institute, George Jones from the London School of Economics and Clive Holtham the Director of Finance from Hammersmith and Fulham, who have all read and commented on the first draft. I owe a special debt to Michael Clarke, the Director of the Local Government Training Board, both for his comments and for his support and encouragement.

Finally, my thanks to my wife for help and support. It is a great advantage for the student of Local Government to be married to a councillor!

# 1

# Introduction

## THE STARTING POINT

This book is based on the position set out in two previous books. In *The Case for Local Government* (Jones and Stewart, 1983), we argued for local government as a political institution constituted for local choice. In a changing society facing complex problems, local government is more, not less, important. The diffusion of power, the diversity of response, the closeness to community, the economy of provision matched to local choice, mean that local government has the potential to contribute much to the system of government of a changing society. For

to meet the complex challenges of our time, our system of government must have the capacity:

- to learn
- to respond
- to change
- to win public loyalty

Our argument is that learning is advanced by a diffusion of power and a diversity of approach, because there is more to learn and greater variety to learn from. Centralism reduces the capacity of learning.

Our argument is that localness brings a capacity to recognise and to respond to problems and issues, because decision-making in the locality is about situations known and is itself more open to pressure.

Our argument is that change comes more easily in organisations on the smaller scale, and can be achieved with greater economy, because it is matched to local need.

Our argument is that, through local government, the public is more easily able to perceive the linkage between taxation and public expenditure, and thus support community provision.

A centralised system of government would have a reduced capacity to learn, to respond, to change and to win the support of the public. Our case is for strong local government.

Our argument is based on the potential of local government compared with central government for the tasks and roles with which we are concerned. Potential is not always realised in practise. Our concern is to establish an approach to local government that will assist the realisation of that potential

(Jones and Stewart, 1983, pp. 7–8)

That book went on to discuss the institutional framework that would best realise that potential.

In *Local Government: The Conditions of Local Choice* (Stewart, 1983), I discussed the extent to which limits were set to that potential not so much by the institutional framework, but by the way that local authorities organised themselves to carry out their work. Local authorities are both agencies for the provision of services and political institutions constituted for local government and capable of local choice. The book argues that most local authorities are more organised for the continuities of service provision than for local government. Organisational limits were set to local choice.

It was, however, recognised in that book that under the pressures of economic and social change, mediated through changing politics, 'the limits of organisational choice can be and have recently been extended' (Stewart, 1983, p. ix), although the extent of organisational change was as yet limited. That is the starting point for this book. It is argued that under the pressures of a changing society, and despite attempts by central government to limit local choice, local authorities are placing a new emphasis on their role as local government, widely concerned with the area they govern and capable of local choice on the activities they undertake. That new emphasis requires new approaches to the ways that local authorities are organised to do their work and there are signs that these approaches are developing. For the role of local government a new management is required.

By management is meant the way a local authority organises itself to carry out its work; how it determines its policies, and how it implements them; how it plans, chooses, influences and acts. As such the new management involves both councillors and officers.

The first part of the book (Chapter 2 to Chapter 4), Part One, sets out the need for that new management by contrast with the traditional management of local government. It restates the position set out in my previous book and suggests that traditional management supported the role of local authorities as providers of services, rather than as political institutions with a capacity for local choice.

A new management is required that can express the values of local government in a changing environment. That is required all the more because local authorities face resource constraint. Choice becomes the more critical. A new management is required too when local authorities are under attack by central government or by the press. It is only as local government that local authorities can justify themselves and that requires management appropriate to that task. This book is a search for what that management might be, drawing examples from newly developing practice, where practice exists (and more examples could be given from other authorities), and setting out ideas for what might yet develop.

This book is designed as an aid to thinking about management in local government. It is a book that asks questions, but does not always give answers. It gives examples to show possibilities, not as models. Those who wish for a fully developed approach will be disappointed. Even if an approach had successfully been developed in a particular authority, the book would not prescribe that as a pattern to be followed by all other authorities. A new management for local government cannot assume a single pattern. Local government is about local choice, not national uniformity.

What is required is not slavish following of a standard pattern, but new thought on the nature of management in local government. The past management of local government has imposed a remarkable degree of uniformity and stability on the organisation of different local authorities. The first need is to challenge organisational assumption and then to stimulate new thinking appropriate to the needs of each local authority.

If the challenge helps those who read it to understand the assumptions they have made, if the stimulus helps them to adopt new approaches to the management of local government, the book will have fulfilled its purpose better than if any particular suggestion is followed. It is a book for thinking, not a guide to action, but that thinking should itself guide action.

## THE UNDERLYING ASSUMPTION

There is one basic assumption made in the book. Local authorities have been constituted to behave in ways that are different from other organisations. Local authorities are public sector organisations, not market organisations. This means that they make different decisions and in different ways from market organisations. They make their decisions subject to political control, rather than market discipline. That is not to be regretted, but to be welcomed. Their responsibilities have presumably been given to local authorities, rather than to the market, because the market does not provide an acceptable basis for decisions on those responsibilities. If it were not so, then the appropriate response is not for local authorities to behave as if they were market organisations, but for those responsibilities to be placed in the market. So long as those responsibilities are subject not to the market but to the political process of local authorities, then it has to be accepted not only that those authorities do, but that they should make their decisions as political and not as market organisations.

Local authorities are not part of central government. This means that they make different decisions and in different ways from central government. They make the local choice, not the national choice. That is not to be regretted but welcomed. If local authorities were merely to make decisions as they would have been made by central government, there is little point in local authorities as separate political institutions. Local authorities have been constituted as local political institutions, based on local elections, close to community pressures, so that they can make a local choice. If it were not so, then the appropriate response is not for local authorities to behave as if they were part of national government, but for their responsibilities to be given to central government. So long as those responsibilities are subject to local choice, then it should be accepted not only that those choices do, but that they should, be made subject to local not national political processes.

The point is that local authorities as local government are constituted to behave not in the same way as, but differently from other organisations. A new management for local government should realise that difference. That is its difficulty but also its excitement. So much of thought about management has been developed for organisations that differ in their conditions and their purposes from local government, that it is easy for management thinking in local authorities to treat the conditions and purposes of local government as of relatively little importance. Thus the politics of local government can well be treated as an incidental feature of local authorities rather than as expressing their purposes. If the local authority were seen merely as a provider of services on well established lines then that may not matter. But a new management that supports the role of local authorities as local government has not merely to accept the politics of local government, but to start from the political processes as giving purpose to the workings of local government.

The excitement of a new management in local government is that it calls for new thinking about the nature of management; it requires management that supports the political processes; it recognises that local choice reflects value choice and responds to the pressures of the local community. Politics, values, pressures are not extraneous to the new management but its conditions and its purposes.

In the second part of the book (Chapter 4 to Chapter 9), management processes, organisational structures and staffing policies for the new management are discussed. Certain themes recur, focussing challenge and change for they set the character of the new management, in contrast to traditional management.

- Political processes define the purposes of local government, and management has to express, not to deny, those processes.
- As local government, the authority seeks the learning of the communities it governs and by which it is governed.
- Yet learning is not enough and there is also choice.
- The authority has to achieve both choice in policy direction and responsiveness in action.
- Beyond action, for local government, there is also influence.
- Choice and responsiveness cannot be confined within past organisational limits.
- But more important than a change in structures or procedures is a change in organisational culture.

The new management for local government will be very different from what the book describes as 'traditional management', conditioned by the continuities of service provision. Learning, choice, flexibility, responsiveness, political are all words dominant in writing on the new management. The language of traditional management uses words such as control, standard, stability, uniformity, profession, function. But a local authority is both a provider of service and local government. A new management does not replace traditional management. Both are required.

This means that as the new management becomes established, there will be a need for organisational understanding and organisational management (also dealt with in Part Two). For the organisational dilemma of a local authority that has both to maintain the reliability of its service and to respond in change to a changing society has to be resolved not at a particular moment of time, but continuously. The task of organisational management is not the management of change, but the management of a changing organisation in a changing environment.

# PART ONE

# A New Management for a Changing Polity

# 2

# Traditional Management for an Established Polity

## THE ESTABLISHED POLITY

The local authority is a provider of services, but it is also a political institution charged with local government. As a provider of services, the activities to be carried out are largely prescribed, if not in statute, then in the past working of the authority. As local government, the local authority has a capacity for local choice on the activities to be undertaken, and a concern for its area that goes beyond the services provided.

Local authorities can become so absorbed in the provision of services that their role as local government can be forgotten. In the post-war years of expenditure growth, with the establishment of the welfare state, the provision of services seemed the dominant, indeed the only, role for local authorities. Each year from 1952 to 1975, local government expenditure grew in real terms, and was expected to grow and to continue to grow, largely fuelled by central government grants and loan sanctions. This growth was not achieved against the wishes of central government, but through its encouragement. Growth in local government expenditure expressed general public aspiration for growing services. There was a confidence in the services and in the need for growth in provision. There was a certainty in the contribution of that provision as there was stability in its organisation. The problems faced by local authorities could be met by growth in existing services, and even where new and emerging problems required new activities, that could be achieved without challenge to existing services. Growth in expenditure provided conditions of stability for local government. The increment of growth provided the means to meet emerging problems without challenge to past practice.

The politics of local government were the politics of consensus.

The politics of local government in that period have been described as more concerned with patronage than policy (Bulpitt, 1967). The parties divided on a limited number of issues such as sale of council houses, and in some but not all education authorities, on comprehensive education. Michael Hill, writing in 1972, was able to say:

> English local government operates in a context of low public interest, a context in which there is little public conflict about policies. Accordingly party political conflict is absent, or muted, too; and so decision-making is largely in the hands of professional administrators.
>
> (Hill, 1972, p. 211)

The politics of consensus was based on acceptance of the universalism of expertise and knowledge. Councillors of all parties had confidence in the services and in the advice given by officers on their development. Officers put their faith in established professional practice. Universal solutions based on expert knowledge were pursued for what were seen as common problems for all local authorities. There was little apparent need for local government or local choice. The role of local authorities was to provide ever growing services, organised on the basis of established expertise. This was the polity of local government accepted by councillors and officers alike.

The dominant values in local authority were those of a passive politics, uniformity of approach and established expertise. These values were expressed in what will be described in this book as the traditional management of local government.

Traditional management was geared to the role of local authorities in providing a well established pattern of service. The dominant features of traditional management were and are:

- the committee setting
- the bureaucratic mode
- the professional culture

Despite the variety that could be local government, those features built a uniformity of management practice across authorities. In the necessities of service provision, the potential of local government was neglected and local choice forgotten. Yet traditional management expressed the polity of the times in which, although already well developed, it gained its strength and its force.

## THE COMMITTEE SETTING

The council formally controls the working of the local authority through the committee system. The committees, constituted by the council, define the work of the departments, making decisions on the policies to be followed and often in considerable detail on the operations to be undertaken to achieve those policies.

The committee system distinguishes the workings of the local authority from those of central government. In central government control over departments is exercised by ministers who gain their formal authority from the Crown and Parliament. In local government control over departments lies with the committees whose formal authority comes from the council. The formal emphasis in local government is on the collective authority of the committee and the council. The chairpersons of the committees have no formal, as opposed to political, authority. They chair the meetings of their committees, and derive such power as they exercise from the committee. Their power to influence and even to instruct officers in departments derives from their ability to secure a majority in the committee, of which with clear political control they can normally be assured. Based on such clear political control, there are signs that some local authorities are moving toward the ministerial model, giving to the chair a degree of authority over the working of the department. Even in such authorities the forms of committee work continue to be observed.

The committee system creates a particular style of decision-making. The formal agendas, reports and procedures condition the working of departments. The existence of committees as the expression of political control can draw upward to their agendas issues which in other forms of organisation could be resolved at lower levels in the officer hierarchy. The committee cycle can come to dominate the working of senior staff in the department. The timetable of the committee becomes the timetable for departmental business and departmental thinking. Agendas are filled up, and reports prepared following well established routines. Thinking about problems and issues can easily be replaced by report writing which can weaken officers' sense of responsibility for their recommendations, 'It's up to the members now; it's their decision.' Yet to members of the committee, their decisions can easily be a mere formality.

A committee can be dominated by the agenda, the formal setting and the routine of business. Committee procedures are not structured for discussion, but for the enactment of formal decisions. A 'good' chair drives the committee from item number one to item number forty (or whatever other number lies at the end of the agenda) without two much trouble on the way. In the pressure of business, ideas can die unheard.

The committee system has clear strengths. Its very formality provides a clear and authoritative basis for decision-making. It ensures councillor involvement in the working of the authority. Committee members have, thereby, legitimate standing in relation to the activities of the departments. The committee is the formal expression of political control over the working of the authority.

However, as the committee system conditions the working of the department, so it also conditions the councillors' approach to their role. Committees – apart from the council – are often the only organisational setting provided by the authority for the work of a councillor. The councillor's role is defined as committee work. In that work the councillor is often involved merely in 'getting through the agenda', which can well be based more on the department's operational requirements rather than on political priorities. The necessities of service provision create their own agenda.

The dominant influence of the committee system involves councillors in the requirements of continuing service provision without providing adequate support for the political process. The task of government is overwhelmed by the detail of decision-making on service provision. The formality of the committee setting prevents proper discussion of service provision.

The committee system influences the working of departments, the role played by councillors and the relationship between them. As the chair speeds from one item to another on the agenda, the opportunity for local government is lost.


## THE BUREAUCRATIC MODE

The local authority provides its services through departments. There is a similarity in the way departments, carrying out very different activities, are organised. The organisation charts match each other, with chief officer and deputy chief officer, and a broad third tier of senior management. Underlying the working of the different departments are three common organising principles, which are so influential, that they can almost be regarded as defining 'sound administration' in local government.

(i) The principle of hierarchy enforces organisational control and arrays staff in a hierarchy of responsibility to the chief officers, and through them to the committee and the council.

(ii) The principle of uniformity enforces formal equality of treatment, and to prescribe that, the policies and practices of the authority are applied in the same way throughout the area of the authority.

(iii) The principle of functionalism enforces the division of the work of the council according to the expertise required, and is given expression in departments based on the main perceived functions of the council.

The principles reinforce each other. The functional departments are organised into hierarchies of responsibility which enforce uniformity within those departments.

The principles had their own necessity as public services grew in scale.

Since the beginning of the twentieth century, social reformers in many fields had sought to replace local charities, the local poor law and local friendly societies with nationwide services. These services were then pressed to adopt increasingly similar practices throughout the country. Official guidance about pupil– teacher ratios, about prescriptions per doctor and per patient, about points systems for the allocation of council housing and about codes for the distribution of social security benefits were all designed to produce greater uniformity. Radicals helped to standardise things. Variety, they argued, created 'anomalies', and anomalies were 'indefensible'. Always alert to seize upon these anomalies as precedents for reform, they compelled government to adopt an increasingly uniform mould in self-defence.

The achievements of this heroic age could perhaps only have been attained by a set of fairly single-minded centralised bureaucracies which focused and confined the energies of politicians and officials within the frontiers of clearly distinguished departments of central and local government. A functional, service-oriented system was created to win the 'numbers games' of these years: to build the houses, to clear the slums, to get the new pensions paid, to ensure there would be a place in school for every five-year-old, to deploy hospital consultants in every region, to build more miles of motorway and to bring down the numbers on the waiting lists. The heroes of these games – the chairmen of housing and education committees, their chief supporters and senior officials – too often became detached from the people on whose behalf they laboured. They thought of these people as tenants, pupils, patients, social work clients, losing sight of the more complex human reality behind the flood of committee papers and the smoke of bureaucratic battles.

(Donnison, 1983, p. 2)

The principles express bureaucracy and have both the strengths and the weaknesses of bureaucracy. They ensure the provision of services according to established rules, but limit variation to meet varying circumstances. They limit the exercise of arbitrary power, but also discretion and responsiveness. Accountability within the hierarchy of responsibility is emphasised, but at the expense of accountability to the client.

The strengths of the principles are their weaknesses, as their weaknesses are their strengths. Impartial application of rules is a strength, but is a weakness if one of the criteria is responsiveness. Uniformity is a strength, but can be a weakness if needs and demands vary. Functional specialism is a strength, but can be a weakness if problems felt and encountered do not match those specialisms. A hierarchy of accountability has the strength of ensuring formal political control, but can be a weakness if, as messages pass up or down the hierarchy, understanding is lost.

The principles are necessary for the large-scale delivery of standard services. The clear and certain application of established rules is, then, a strength in unchanged circumstances. That assumes, however, that the service provided is the service required, and will remain the service required. If the focus is on local government, then that cannot be assumed. The rules may not fit the changing world to which they are applied.

The principles restrict learning to that which falls within established functional divides, and can climb the long hierarchies, dividing fieldworkers from the centre of the authority. The principles restrict the capacity to respond to the variety of needs and problems that exist in the field, and to learn from that variety in response. The principles restrict the organisational capacity for change to those changes that can be made throughout the authority, and prevent the learning that comes from diversity.

The principles are, of course, modified in practice. Informal does not always confine itself to the formal. Practices vary more than can be ensured by any hierarchy of control. Individuals do not limit their role to their formal responsibilities.

The principles remain the norm and, as such, deeply influence the organisational culture of local authorities. Departures from them require special justification, if they cannot be hidden in the informal working of the organisation.

• When new local authorities were established in 1974, often bringing together very different areas, almost their first act, after having established their hierarchical structure, was to consider how to develop uniform policies throughout the authority. The principle of uniformity ruled out consideration of the possibility that policies varied between constituent authorities because needs and problems or wishes and demands varied. Uniformity had to be sought, although it was not easily established.

- 'How can I say to councillors that I disagree with my chief's views?' In many authorities such actions would be regarded as an act of administrative disloyalty. The principle of hierarchy prevails over the learning that comes from differences of view.
- At the reception desk of the town hall, the many dimensioned problems expressed by the public are squeezed into the rigidities of the functional divides. A problem must be a housing, social services or education problem, it cannot be allowed to be the problem seen by the individual in front of the desk. The functional principle sets its own organisational constraints.

The principles have become written into the thought processes of those who work within the local authorities. They have become not principles, the application of which can be discussed, but assumptions that are rarely challenged.

## A PROFESSIONAL CULTURE

The officer structure of local government is based on professionalism. In each department of a local authority there is a dominant profession. The chief officer and most of the senior staff of that department are drawn from that profession. The work carried out by the profession is regarded as the key task of the department.

A profession moulds those who belong to it. They share skills backed by specialist knowledge and attitudes about their clients and their environment. The profession draws its approach from a shared theoretical framework and conducts itself according to professional ethics which may be expressed in a formal code. Professionalism is reinforced by a systematic process of common training and qualification, and is maintained by professional associations. Professional training has been a major formative influence on most of the senior staff of local government. The profession sustains the loyalty of its members. Most professionals in local government, if asked their occupation, would reply, 'architect', 'librarian' or 'solicitor' rather than 'local government officer'.

The dominant profession in a local authority department

inevitably sets the culture of that department, determining the values stressed and the favoured approaches towards its activities. The language of the profession becomes the language of the department, whether it is the 'caring sharing' language of social work or the precise language of accountancy.

The dominant profession's assumptive world, involving 'perceptions of the world, evaluations of its aspects, a sense of relatedness to them, and recurrent demands that they be acted upon' (Young and Kramer, 1978, p. 228) provides the basis upon which the department works. Because this assumptive world is shared, it need not even be stated. Its power lies deeper than words spoken or written. It is ingrained.

The dominant profession shapes the culture of the department, but some within the department will not easily accept it. There can be tensions between the dominant profession and other staff who do not automatically accept the perceived pretensions of the professional. There can be tensions between administrative and professional staff in departments. There are subordinate professions or semi-professions such as education welfare officers in education or occupational therapists in social services departments, who may consider their contribution undervalued and their career prospects blocked. If there is a departmental culture based on the dominant profession, there may also be subdepartmental counter cultures.

The model of the department with a dominant profession is the norm in local government. There is, however, variation in practice. The status of some professions is not as securely established as others. In housing departments it is not uncommon to find chief officers who are not members of the Institute of Housing and may have come from other departments. There are combined departments drawing together professions from previously separate departments, as with the recently formed leisure and recreation departments. In such departments there is a move to form a new profession of leisure and recreation managers, thus reinforcing the dominance of the normative model of department and linked profession. Computer managers have recently formed a Society of Information Technology Managers in Local Government. They, like many others, have taken the first step on the road towards the formation of a new local government profession. The model is there for all to follow.

The working of local government is deeply influenced by professionalism. That professionalism brings great strengths. It brings skills and knowledge related to the main services to be provided. It brings, too, a deep commitment to those services. The engineer takes pride in his roads. The education officer believes in the contribution of the schools to society. Each profession has a clear focus on the services with which it is concerned. The shared assumptive world can eliminate the need for detailed control over professional activities. Professionals can be trusted to provide the services they are trained for.

These strengths, however, assume that the main task of the local authority is the continuing delivery of services along the pattern determined by professionalism. The professional model has been a force for stability rather than for change. Margaret Simey, the chair of the Merseyside Police Committee, wrote:

> The growth in specialism and spreading ambition to achieve the independence and prestige of professionalism have meant that the original political purpose has given way to a concentration on the service rather than on those served.
>
> (Simey, 1985, p. 5)

One does not have to accept the word 'ambition' to recognise the force in the argument. While it would certainly be wrong to argue that professionalism has ruled out change, it will favour developments within established professional boundaries. If a local authority wished to create a new general purpose environmental inspectorate, the barrier would be the existing professions and the divisions between them. The dominant professional perspective can prevent the development of alternative perspectives.

Professions have their own values which can run counter to political values in an authority. The training of a professional is in uniformity of practice, in professional standards, and in attitudes which place greater weight on the profession than on the local authority or its political purposes. The professional is socialised to believe less in the importance of local government and its political processes and more in the importance of the profession. The bias in training can be overcome, but only with an effort, rarely made by traditional management.

Professionalism is a strength in the provision of established services, but that very strength can restrict the exercise of local choice that is the role of local authorities as local government.

## CONCLUSION

Traditional management was well suited to the polity of local government in the post-war period of expenditure growth. There was a passive politics reflecting consensus on the accepted professional solution, a confidence in the pattern of services provided and a belief in a universality of approach, which limited the perception of difference and diversity. Traditional management supported these values in the working of local authorities.

Traditional management has three bases:

- the committee setting
- the bureaucratic mode
- the professional culture

Bureaucracy with its hierarchical authority combines with professional authority in ways that reflect the limited local choice of a passive politics.

Traditional management has great strengths for the delivery of a uniform pattern of service. It met the requirement of a polity confident in the services provided and in the expertise underlying them.

While traditional management supported the role of local authorities in the continuity of service provision, it gave little support for the role of local authorities as political institutions constituted for local choice.

- The political process was confined to committee agendas dominated by the necessities of continuing service provision.
- In the long hierarchies of control, learning for government could be lost.
- In the certainties of uniformity, the choices found in difference could be hidden.
- Problems were fitted to the functional divisions, because the divisions were assumed to match reality.
- The certainties of professionalism may not allow for the changing politics of a changing world.
- The very strengths of traditional management for continuing service provision can be its weaknesses for local government.

The polity expressed in traditional management is challenged by a changing society. As the polity of local government changes, traditional management becomes a constraint upon the capacity of councillors and officers. While its strengths are still required, its weaknesses have to be overcome.

# 3

# Governing in a Turbulent Environment

## THE EROSION OF STABILITY

The apparently stable conditions upon which the established polity of local government rested have been challenged by the ending of the era of growth and by the uncertainties of a turbulent environment.

With intensifying national economic problems in the 1970s, the era of growth came to an end. Central government moved from the encouragement of expenditure growth to demands for constraint and cutback. The party was over, or so cruelly and unfairly it was said.

Central government could act directly on capital expenditure. Revenue expenditure could not be directly controlled by central government, but only indirectly influenced by reduction in grant and by exhortation. Over the period since 1974/5 successive governments reduced the share of rate borne expenditure supported by grant from 66.5 per cent (England and Wales) in 1974/5 to under 50 per cent in 1985/6 (England only). The Conservative government elected in 1979 developed a variety of grant mechanisms designed to ensure that local authorities met its plans for expenditure reduction. In 1984, the Conservative government took direct powers under the Rates Act to control directly the expenditure and taxing decisions of selected local authorities, with general powers held in reserve.

Local government expenditure has not fallen to the extent sought by central government, which always seemed to demand greater reductions in local government expenditure than it was ready to impose on itself (Jones and Stewart, 1983). Nevertheless, there has been a change. The period since 1974/5 has been a period of constraint, whether that constraint was a result of the changed economic climate, government persuasion, grant reduction or the gradual accumulation of central government's powers. Local authorities varied in their response; in some, severe cuts were made in expenditure; in others, expenditure grew for at least part of the period. But in all, the climate had changed, and growth in expenditure year by year could no longer be regarded as the normal condition of local government.

Growth in expenditure provided the basis for the established polity. There was a sense of achievement in new buildings and growing services. Growth appeared to justify existing patterns of service, as public pressure appeared to demand growth in those services.

The era of constraint has undermined the confidence given by growth, which has been replaced by new uncertainties. In an era of constraint, conflicts deepen, whether between departments, between political parties, or between the authority and its public. If growth had been a condition of stability, then constraint destabilised.

In constraint the local authority has lost a capacity for change to meet emerging problems in the environment. Emerging problems can no longer be met out of growing resources; change now involves challenge to existing patterns of service provision, and, in the end, hard choices.

## AN UNCERTAIN SOCIETY

The local authority carries out its activities in a world of uncertainty. In part there is uncertainty in the authority itself, induced by change from growth to constraint. A local authority, stable and sure in its own activities, and in its capacity to deal with emerging problems, imposes its own certainties on the environment.

In part, the uncertainty lies in the environment itself. Economic problems have destroyed confidence in past certainties. Each service provided by the local authority has been challenged. Successes are not easily found in an uncertain society, conscious of economic decline. The perceived failure of urban redevelopment, the economic decay of the inner city, the disappointment of educational performance, the dilemmas of urban transport, the problems of rural isolation, are symptoms of that uncertainty. The aspiration to growing services has been replaced by doubt as to their past impact and as to present and future direction. In economic growth new certainties might have been found, but in economic stagnation and in constraint, solutions are not easily established.

There is, however, a deeper sense of uncertainty that derives from the changing society. The changes faced by local authorities are massive and would, in any event, have challenged the established polity.

The context of local government is being transformed by a more heightened period of social, economic and political change. The causes of these changes are often quite independent of each other, yet they combine to make the world we are moving into very different from that to which we have been more accustomed. Unemployment is raising fundamental questions about the nature of work; social trends show an ageing society, more fragmented patterns of family life often reflecting the changing relations between men and women; a multi-cultural society striving for equality of opportunity; while a more politicised world emerged as conceptions about ways of resolving economic and social problems sharpen.

(Local Government Training Board, 1985, p. 2.)

In these terms a paper prepared by staff from the Local Government Training Board and the Institute of Local Government Studies, after widespread consultations with local authorities, summed up 'the management challenge for local government'. Over and above financial problems, the paper identified:

- the ending of growth
  'the post-war period of economic growth came to an end in the mid 1970s'
- structural changes in employment
  'the challenge of unemployment and its differential impact on local communities'
  'the application of new technologies'
- demographic change
  'the major population problem which Britain faces is of an ageing society'
- dependency and poverty
  'the dependent population of young and old has increased considerably over the last two decades'
- social change
  'the changing position of women and the changed experience of family life'
- political change
  'the changing context is creating a more political world'
  (Local Government Training Board, 1985)

While the Local Government Training Board study looked at the changing context of the present, a study by the Futures Panel of the

Society of Local Authority Chief Executives (SOLACE) looked to the future. Like much Futures work the report may be a better indication of the nature of present than of future change – for we have no guide, save our imagination, to the future, except that which we find in the past and the present.

If one had to identify a main theme or message for the Society out of the essays produced for the Panel, it is the fact of continuing crisis and uncertainty. A world of work in which:-

a) the rate of change will continue to accelerate;
b) the gap beteeen the haves and the have nots could well continue to widen not only in international terms but also on the domestic scene. Brandt cannot be ignored for ever;
c) divisions and differences between territorial units within the United Kingdom could widen;
d) the fuel crisis is likely to return;
e) other shortages will emerge as population continues to increase and demands expand. The benefits of the "green revolution" are finite and important mineral shortages are forecast;
f) new technology will have unforseeable consequences for employment, for service delivery, and for working practices;
g) the burden of an increasingly ageing population will expand demands on already finite resources;
h) attitudes towards leisure and work will undergo a profound change;
i) the problems of care and women will continue to be important but, to an extent, peripheral issues.

(Society of Local Authority
Chief Executives, 1985, pp. 14–15)

The hesitation in the last item reflects the degree of challenge to past modes of organisational thought and practice by emerging social forces. Those past modes are not easily changed even by those who accept the need for change.

There can be no definitive list of the changes in society faced by local authorities. Increasingly, however, those within local authorities are becoming deeply aware of the extent of those changes. Whether it is SOLACE considering the future, or the Local Government Training Board analysing the changing context, there is the same recognition of the challenges involved. Those challenges are to the established polity. They cannot be met merely by the maintenance of the existing pattern of services.

Economic change, whether that involves decline or restructuring, challenges the local authority to new initiatives, unrestricted by past organisational ways of working. Many local authorities experience high unemployment in their community. Others in relatively prosperous areas fear its threat. Few authorities have not looked beyond existing services, to new approaches to assist the local economy, breaking through organisational precedent and the cautions of past practice. New relations with the private sector; new attempts to stimulate small businesses or to build co-operatives; and new opportunities for community initiatives may be difficult to reconcile with past norms of public accountability, in which risk was unacceptable. Yet a local authority that feels accountable for the general welfare of the local community will see such initiatives as part of its role.

The scope for direct local authority action is limited, and the impact is small in relation to the scale of unemployment. Endemic unemployment bears most heavily upon the young, and can scar communities beyond the present. Local authorities cannot avoid concern for present and future unemployment. Services built in an era of full employment may be based on assumptions that no longer apply. A local authority is challenged to reappraisal – not least of its own personnel policies – for it is likely to be one of the largest employers, if not the largest, in its area. If the boundary between work and non-work has to change, local authorities' own employment policies can begin to show the way.

New technology presents one aspect of economic change, but involves more than economic change. It can have an effect on levels of employment, but also on the conditions of employment. Home-based employment can grow, smaller units of employment develop, and new locations become possible. Existing transportation and planning policies are based on the assumption of past technologies. New technology can also have a direct impact on the management of local authorities, making possible new forms of decentralisation to neighbourhood offices, with information directly available to client or customer.

Social patterns are changing. Unemployment itself is a cause of change, but other changes are taking place. The growth of divorce, the increasing number of one-parent families and new life styles challenge many of the assumptions on which existing patterns of service provision are based. The lines of division in our society become more marked – between the employed and the unemployed, between inner city and suburb, between the opportunities available to men and to women, or for those with differing ethnic backgrounds, between the North of decline and the South of economic growth, between the cultures of young and of old – not because the lines necessarily grow deeper, but because they become serious in their implications without the hope of employment.

Awareness of difference and division may lead to policies that vary with the needs faced. To treat all the same may lead to formal equality, but formal equality may lead to actual inequity. Such is the lesson of a multi-racial society.

Differing needs are not met by a common response, but by a capacity to respond to and through difference. On issues as varied as curriculum in schools, care of the aged and book selection in libraries, the services will fail to meet felt need if ethnic dimensions are not recognised. Discrimination has to be identified as recognised in a report by the chief executive of Leicester.

> The central feature is that ethnicity belongs to the individual ... whilst discrimination is imposed upon the individual ...
>
> Certain services are required to respond to ethnicity in specific ways ... but other services may be treating people in a discriminating way by assuming that some behaviour results from ethnicity rather than as a consequence of unequal opportunity and discrimination.
>
> (Leicester, 1982)

The issues arise sharply on the achievement of equal opportunities in a local authorities own employment policies. As Ken Young has put it:

> Does equal opportunity denote the equal *treatment* of people from different ethnic groups or their achievement of equal *shares* of that scarce good, employment? Such ambiguity is not unique to the discussion of equal opportunity.
>
> (Young, 1984, p. 3)

In a later article he argued that:

> It would seem that many elected members are looking to current adaptations in policy and practice to produce 'equal shares', often seen as ethnic proportionality in employment: they interpret 'equal opportunity' as equality of *outcomes*. Other participants in local authority decision-making, and perhaps personnel specialists in particular, see the problem as one of achieving equal treatment: that is, establishing procedures which ensure that decisions on recruitment, promotion or redundancy are taken in accordance with criteria that are fair, relevant and lawful.
>
> (Young, 1984, p. 16)

Uniformity of policy and practice can ensure equal treatment. More may be required to ensure equal shares.

The economic and social environment changes, but so does the physical environment and concern for that environment. The ecologist's agenda is becoming more widely accepted. New scarcities can challenge old securities. Pollution can spread; the appearance of the countryside changes.

This book, however, attempts no comprehensive survey of change in society. The purpose lies not in the listing, but in the significance of societal change in a period when local authorities have lost their means of change through growth. The changes in society contain no certainties of the future. Awareness of rapid change does not build a sense of certainty, but of uncertainty. The certainty of the task of service provision is being replaced by an awareness that the task of local authorities is the government of uncertainty – both uncertainty in the nature of the problems to be faced and uncertainty as to their solutions.

## THE NEW POLITICS

The politics of local government change in a changing environment. The political process links the authority directly to the environment, for politicians gain their authority from the community. The political process can be insulated from its environment only at a cost, which few wish to incur. Politics is the process of intermediation between societal change and governmental action.

The ending of the era of growth and the challenges of a changing society have been expressed in a new and assertive politics. Even before the era of constraint public confidence in the existing patterns of service provision was beginning to wane and with it political support for the consensus on the established professional solution.

In an era of continuing economic growth coupled with rising local government expenditure a new consensus might have been found, although there were signs in society generally of a decline in acceptance – not least of government action. Road lines drawn on maps faced expectation of ever increasing protest. Public protest grew ever greater around school closures or housing clearance. A politics of protest had begun to articulate hostility to imposed public action to which the political processes of the local authority responded.

Political change has been rapid. An immediate effect of the 1974 local government reorganisation was the spread of party politics and the establishment of a base for the new assertive politics. In part those changes were associated with reorganisation itself. The merging of urban with rural politics in the shire counties; the abolition of aldermen, removing from the council senior members protected from the political processes of elections; and the introduction of attendance allowances as a form of payment to councillors encouraged the development of the new politics.

That new politics has developed rapidly in the era of constraint and in a changing society. Local authorities, which had sought in the fifties and the sixties to build the golden city, knew that it had not been built, but there was uncertainty now as to what should be built. If there was uncertainty as to the changes taking place, there was also uncertainty as to the response. The remaining basis for consensus died in the new uncertainty.

Instead of consensus there was increasing difference between the political parties at local as at national level. The local parties differed on expenditure policies – not merely on whether cuts should be made but on the nature of those cuts.

The new politics challenged the established polity that supported the continuing provision of the past pattern of services and challenged also the ways of working through which that polity can be expressed. Examples can be drawn from all parties. The Conservative leader of Taunton Deane District Council described the approach applied in that authority:

> We asked ourselves whether the profile of Taunton Deane Council committees and departments closely matched the profile and needs of the community. The answer we got was that the Council profile (like human nature) had not changed in decades! We had too slavishly credited our predecessors with a wisdom which would not stand up to changing economic and social structure. In short we had a disparity between our structure, and the needs of the people. Back to the drawing board, our priorities as we saw them were firstly the economy and employment situation, secondly the encouragement of the voluntary field of activities, and thirdly the routine statutory duties concerned with hygiene, health, highways, playing fields, planning permission, etc., etc. If these were our priorities, then where was the powerful economic committee or panel, where was the effort being put into tourism? Were we changing the emphasis of Officers giving time to those newer and important activities? Over two and a half years we changed the structure of Officers, Committees and Departments of the Council.
>
> (Meikle, 1984, p. 8)

Or again:

> Taunton Deane accepts this new presumption that Local Government services are not sacrosanct. If some existing services could be

transferred to the private sector, which previously had been held on habit and convention, this would enable us to complete our profile as a district council looking towards the nineties. Members and Officers could be released to devote time assisting the economy, tourism and the general promotion of voluntary activities within Taunton Dean.

(Meikle, 1984, p. 10)

David Blunkett, the Labour leader of Sheffield, has made many statements challenging not merely the existing policies of local authorities but their way of working:

The problem is more specifically why *personal social services* have not got the commitment of people in the community. One reason is the way we have delivered services, whether they be in Services Departments, Housing, Education, Recreation, or Transport. We have, in fact, 'delivered' them. We have not provided services *with* people, we have provided them for people. Therefore our commitment has been to some sort of paternalistic socialism where we say 'Give us a chance and we will do it for you'. We have done that at national level and we have done it at local level and we end up being defensive. We are defensive about the role of tenants in housing, defensive about the role of parents and teachers, and we end up defensive about the role of so-called 'clients'. Central and local Government services end up being something given to people out of the grace of our good hearts and not something they are participating in and feel to be theirs.

If we are seriously going to talk about getting a coherent policy, we need to talk about the way we deliver what it is that we are supposed to be doing on behalf of the people. As Socialists, we need to think about the relationship of those we employ with the community for whom they work and we need to examine the relationship of those who are elected to represent that community with those same people. The interface between the people who are getting something and those who are delivering it, either as elected members or as paid workers, is vital.

If we take Social Services as an example, then perhaps we could examine how to deal with the provision of services for the elderly. Take the provision of old people's homes. Are they somewhere that is separate and isolated from the community in which they are placed, a kind of retreat that people are put into when they are no longer able to cope in their own homes, away from their friends, neighbours and family on whom they normally relied in what we now call the 'community network'! Or is a community home literally that — an actual part of the community, a living part, where people are coming in and out, helping, supporting. They are not replacing staff – they are giving that additional ability to treat people as human beings and not as clients. Are day centres places where adult education is taking place, where people are coming in and out to deliver things or are they places where people are delivered by our community transport, left for a good lunch and a warm, and then collected again and taken home? Both those things are valuable, but they are less valuable if they are being done in isolation.

(Blunkett, 1981, pp. 97–99)

Alliance councillors, too, see themselves challenging past ways of working, with the Liberals stressing the contribution of community politics. In their publication 'Local Open and Efficient', the Association of Liberal Councillors outlined changes required, not merely in patterns of service provision but in ways of working:

At the heart of our proposals is the commitment to develop community government. This idea has many facets, but the intention is to bring local government far closer to ordinary people, to remove much of the mystique which surrounds it, and in this way rejuvenate what has become an increasingly remote and jaded institution. We want to see County Councils increasingly working with community groups and voluntary organisations within different communities not, as the Tories would do, to use them as cheap labour to save money. This would release the vast energy and potential found in such organisations so that the whole community can benefit and the quality of life improves instead of remaining static or deteriorating.

A shift to Smaller Areas

We want to see decentralisation of local authority departments to smaller areas within the Counties, matched by area committees composed of Councillors and, where possible, community representatives. These committees would have spending powers within an overall budget set by the County and would control activities in their own area.

(Association of Liberal Councillors, 1985)

These statements from all parts of the political spectrum could be multiplied many times over. There is a shared critique of past forms of service provision, although no consensus on the response. There is a shared challenge to the definition of need by the organisation with too little regard for the views of those for whom it is provided.

In response some emphasise consumer sovereignty achieved through the market, leading to proposals for privatisation and greater use of fees and charges. Some emphasise a growth in self-help and voluntary service. Others emphasise community control achieved through new decentralised structures, community groups and new forms of involvement in decision-making by the deprived.

The new politics has also brought in some authorities a concern for equal opportunities, which has exposed the institutional discrimination present in local government. Unstated organisational assumptions may be the source of institutional discrimination, as when informal recruitment practices (as opposed to the use of job centres and advertisements) for manual and clerical workers reproduce the workforce's existing racial mix. The Women's Committees in Newcastle, Camden and Lewisham identified the youth service 'as geared almost exclusively to boys' (Webster, 1983, p. 32) and those conclusions could doubtless be replicated in many other authorities.

The new politics has brought, to some authorities, consideration of how market forces can break through the 'protectionism' of local authorities leading them to greater use of competitive tendering for such services as refuse disposal and school cleaning. These ideas have been given legislative support in relation to direct labour organisations and as this book is being written further legislation is contemplated.

In these and in other ways the new politics is transforming the assumptive world of local authorities. The framework of ideas that supported the role of local authorities as providers of a well established pattern of services is challenged in the political process.

The political process continues to change. Local electoral choice has widened as the Alliance parties have increased their representation on councils, coming to actual control in only a few authorities but holding the balance in a growing number. The safety of majority control has been changed into the new uncertainties of decision-making in a hung authority, and further sets of political ideas have to be taken into account.

Nor are the changing politics of local government confined to politics within the authority. Change in politics is itself a response to changes in society, and changes are found in a new politics of the community. The politics surrounding local authorities encompasses a politics of pressure and protest. It involves community groups, chambers of commerce, ethnic groups, women's groups, residents' associations and groups that emerge to campaign against a particular proposal. Always present, such groups have grown in importance in the politics of local authorities.

In a turbulent environment the politics of the party and the politics of the community have changed. Yet there is no single pattern. Politics belongs to the locality and can vary with the locality. There are many styles of Labour parties and of Labour groups. There are Conservative authorities that still have the independent tradition of the former shires: there are 'wets' and 'drys'. There are many different ways of being hung. The new politics leads not to uniformity, but provides a challenge to past uniformities based on the acceptance of the existing pattern of service provision.

## NEW ROLES AND NEW WAYS OF WORKING

Under the pressure of resource constraint, challenged by a changing environment, directed by a new politics, assumptions which underlay the working of local authorities are being undermined:

- a local authority role is to provide services;
- those services will be provided directly through its own organisation;
- those services will be provided by its own staff and financed from its own resources.

The local authorities are learning that government in a turbulent environment cannot be so restricted:

- a local authority may influence rather than act directly;
- a local authority may assist individuals or groups to meet needs themselves rather than meet those needs by direct service provision;
- a local authority may secure the provision of the service through the use of other organisations or agencies;
- a local authority may seek new sources of finance from other organisations and agencies;
- a local authority may form partnerships with other organisations and agencies rather than provide a service directly itself.

These developments challenge the model of the self-sufficient authority directly providing service through its own organisation. In a turbulent environment, local authorities are finding new roles and new ways of working. Services which were formerly provided directly by local authorities may now be provided through private contractors. Amongst examples are the refuse collection service in Southend and street cleansing in Wandsworth. The *Local Government Chronicle* regularly surveys the extent of developments (*Local Government Chronicle*, 5.7.1985).

Under the impact of the legislation on direct labour organisations, local authorities open work up to competitive tendering (Flynn and Walsh, 1982). Local authorities have entered into partnerships with the private sector to undertake new developments. Thanet District Council is developing a ferry terminal and Wychavon has secured the re-opening of the Droitwich brine baths by co-operation with the private sector (Wychavon, 1985). An entrepreneurial approach in seeking resources has replaced the certainties of service provision.

Local authorities faced with growing unemployment have accepted a role of community leadership in mobilising financial, economic and social resources from many agencies and organisations. Clwyd County Council faced with the closure of Shotton steelworks drew together many agencies in an alleviation programme which had both a social and an economic dimension (Nott, 1982).

Local authorities in general have taken many initiatives in economic development. Such initiatives necessarily involve work through other agencies and organisations – private companies, worker co-operatives and community groups. While Lancashire County Council set up Lancashire Enterprises Limited, Kent County Council has set up a Kent Economic Development Board.

Local authorities have assisted groups in the community to create projects or to provide services themselves, rather than have the project created or the service provided for them. In Brent, the local authority has helped the Harlesden People's Community Council convert a disused bus garage into a community complex comprising an information technology training centre, under 5s centre, workshops, sports halls and other facilities. In Gloucestershire, the County Council have helped local rural communities to adopt a 'self-help' approach to the improvement of rural services. In Moreton-in-Marsh a Rural Action Project led to, amongst other initiatives, the inauguration of the 'Villager' minibus organised and manned by volunteers.

Local authorities have transferred housing estates to other agencies to run. In Knowsley, the Stockbridge Village Trust was formed as a non-profit-making company to buy the Cantrill Farm Estate, a neglected overspill estate. The Trust is a non-profit-making private company on the Board of which the local authority, the local community and the private companies backing it are represented.

Local authorities have introduced user control of facilities provided by local authorities. The East Cambridgeshire District Council has handed over the management of its leisure centres to local users on a self-financing basis. Local authority housing management co-operatives have been established in Tower Hamlets and in Birmingham (Downey *et al.*, 1982). Other examples are given in the annual survey of public involvement in local government published by the Community Projects Foundation (Smith, 1985).

Local authorities have taken initiatives on women's issues or ethnic issues and against other forms of discrimination. The committees and units involved are not normally engaged in direct service provision, but with expressing the demands of those groups and their implications for the working of the authority. The Southwark Women's Committee has worked on such issues as women's safety, housing allocation and housing design (Goss, 1984). In Hackney an ethnic programme has set targets to bring the numbers of ethnic groups employed by the authority up to the proportion of the borough population belonging to those groups.

Local authorities have recognised that they have a concern for the activities of other agencies in their area and have formed commitees, panels or units to express that concern. The London Borough of Greenwich has set up a Health Sub-Committee (of its Community Affairs Committee) which has within it its terms of reference the consideration of 'all matters relating to health in Greenwich'.

To these few examples, many could be added illustrating new roles and new ways of working. Despite (or possibly because of) the growing constraints on local authorities, initiative and innovation flourish. It is no longer assumed that local authorities can only act through direct service provision. Local authorities are learning ways of governing in a turbulent environment.

A new polity is emerging that supports the role of local authorities as local government constituted for local choice as well as their role in the maintenance of services. The development of that polity can be constrained by traditional management. A new management is required to express the values of the new polity.

## CONCLUSION

The polity of local authorities is changing in a changing world. It is no longer sufficient for local authorities to see their role merely as providers of services, nor to assume that past patterns of service provision are adequate to present and future problems. The pressures of constraint expose the necessity of local choice in a changing and uncertain society. Many local authorities have accepted a concern for their area that goes beyond services provided. The politics of local authorities has expressed these changes, challenging past roles and past ways of working. Local authorities are rediscovering a role as local government. Perhaps local authorities are relearning what they should always have remembered. They are providers of services, but they are also local government. As providers of services, local authorities are administrative conveniences; as local government they are political institutions, justifying local democracy.

Local authorities face the task of governing in an uncertain society. Problems are changing and there is little sureness of their solution. In many ways, this recognition of uncertainty can be healthier for government than sureness and certainty. The government of an uncertain society places a premium on political institutions that have a capacity to learn both of problems and opportunities and of the impact of government; to adapt to the learning; and to bring into effect the changes required. Local authorities bring to the system of government a high capacity for learning. They can be close to the governed. They can constitute the government of difference responding to and creating it – and learning comes from difference not uniformity. Their scale should give a greater capacity for change and innovation than in central government. These capacities, always required, were not sufficiently realised when their role was seen as service provision alone.

Local government involves, however, more than learning and responsiveness to learning. It involves local choice reflecting values held and pursued. There is local choice in response but there is also local choice in direction, both exercised through the political process.

In a new polity the capacity for responsiveness and for choice are being sought. That new polity cannot be adequately expressed by traditional management. As traditional management supported the role of local authorities as service providers, so should a new management support the role of government in a changing society. As traditional management expressed the values of a passive politics, universal provision and expertise of knowledge, so must a new management express the values of the new polity.

- In the new situation of constraint choices have to be faced that in the past could be resolved by growth.
- As the certainties of the past dissolve, learning has to be found in uncertainty.
- Politics changes as society changes and in that changing past ways of working are challenged.
- In new ways of working, local authorities find that they are more than service providers and that there are new modes of service provision.

Local authorities are finding they have a role as local government and require a new management to support that role. Traditional management restrains that role. Both councillors and officers have to break out of the constraints they have imposed upon themselves.

# 4

# The Values of the New Management

## ORGANISATIONAL VALUES

The values required for local government are neglected by traditional management. The new management establishes new values so that local authorities can be more than service providers.

The values to be established and developed within the culture of the new management will vary from authority to authority and with the politics of the authority. Because the values derive from the diversity that is local government the values pursued by the authority will reflect the politics of the council and of the community it governs. In that simple proposition lies the dilemma and the excitement of the new management for local government. In those local authorities where political control changes the values to be emphasised by the authority may change. A local authority which under Conservative control expresses the values of the private sector in commitments to privatisation may become after election day an authority expressing the values of direct public provision. The local authority has to have a capacity to express different values at different times.

A distinction can be made between the values the authority pursues in its policies and those that are written into the continuing working of the organisation. The former are policy values and the latter organisational values. While not entirely distinct, since policy values and organisational values can interact particularly where a continuity of policy develops, organisational values are less likely to be subject to change than policy values.

It is inappropriate to build permanent policy values which reflect the particular purposes of the controlling party when that control may change. An authority has to have a high capacity to accept and pursue changed political purposes. Without that capacity the possibility of political change, which is inherent in local government, becomes a source of confusion and of frustration. What requires to be built are organisational values that support positive responses to political change in policy values.

This chapter sets out organisational values neglected by traditional management which have to be developed by the new management. They may not all need to be developed in each authority; and in each authority they will be given a particular character – for the new management is concerned with the diversity of local government not with the uniformities of national systems. Organisational values can reflect that diversity.

Organisational values are not established merely by reiteration. They are given meaning in action. In presenting possible organisational values for the new management, their meaning is illustrated by the actions they might generate, for those values imply change in the practices of traditional management.

## LOCAL GOVERNMENT

The new management places a value on local government itself. Diffusion of power, diversity of response, and closeness to local community justify the institution of local government.

This much neglected value challenges attitudes deeply inculcated by traditional management. 'National guidelines' or 'accepted professional standards' become for local government, not arguments for a policy, but irrelevancies to be disregarded. Policies would have to be shown to be relevant locally not nationally.

Argument based on an assumed search for uniformity, beyond the requirements of statute, would be unacceptable to the new management. The use of inter-authority comparison as a tool of management would emphasise the value of learning from policy differences and not assume the desirability of the average.

The processes of professional socialisation need to be complemented by processes setting out the rationale for local government. The Local Government Training Board has developed training material to meet this need (LGTB, 1984). Previously little or no training material had been developed on the case for local government, as opposed to routine material on the institutional structure of local government. In traditional management the rationale for local government was irrelevant to the routines of service provision.

Concern for the value of local government means an organisational emphasis on the local election as the basis for the legitimacy of local government. Local elections matter to management. Low and decreasing turn-out should be felt as a sign of organisational weakness. The local authority could develop publicity material, contact with the press and media to improve turn-out, as Cambridgeshire County Council has developed material to attract candidates. 'The public are electors', could be the message reinforced to staff.

If local government had been an organisational value of local authorities, it would not have been possible for central government to prescribe the formal annual reports now required from local authorities under the Local Government, Planning and Land Act 1980. Local authorities would already have been accounting for their activities in forms that took them far beyond annual reports. For to strengthen local accountability is to strengthen local government, not least in its relations with central government.

Local government as an organisational value could be reflected in its working. If local authorities value the diffusion of power to local government, then they, too, can encourage a diffusion of power to users, consumers, tenants, clients and to community groups. If local authorities value diversity of response then they can encourage diversity within. If local authorities value closeness to the local community, then their own procedures should bring them close to the communities within.

## THE POLITICAL PROCESS

The new management places value on the political process which gives expression to the rationale of local government. The political process is a means of making value choice and determining conflict between different interests. It provides the link between governed and government and directs the local authority.

Staff throughout the authority must be aware of the importance of the political process. Concern for the value of the political process requires an emphasis in all staff training on the nature of politics, on political awareness and on political understanding.

Concern for the value of the political process means that a change in political control would be seen not as a disturbance, but as normal working. The possibility of political change would be prepared for. In traditional management, change in political control barely leaves a mark on the agenda of committees or council. Where value was placed on the political process, the nature of any political change would dominate council or committee at meetings immediately after the change. The manifesto of the incoming party or equivalent policy statement would be the main business. As the council's life proceeds, there would be reports on the progress made in achieving the policies of the majority party, reviewing and where necessary re-directing. In hung authorities, the manifestos of the different parties would be a focus for discussion and comparison to establish common ground and areas of disagreement.

Reports to committees would be grounded in political understanding. Politics challenges the unitary model of society which underlies the uniformities of traditional management. Who gains and who loses should not be ignored in presenting a report, and a budget can be presented as an exercise in redistribution. Political decisions would be welcomed. A political rejection of an officer's recommendation is not an irritating interference, but the political process working well.

Staff must understand the policies of the majority party. Councillors from the majority party can play a role in this process, meeting staff, holding discussions with them, and circulating policy statements. Where there is no majority party in a hung authority, staff must be sensitive to political complexity and varying decisions. Whether changing in its political control, continuous in one party or a hung authority, concern for the value of the political process requires an understanding amongst staff of the council's political purposes.

## COMMUNITY RESPONSIBILITY

A value is placed by the new management on responsibility to and for the community. The services are seen not as ends in themselves or merely the fulfilment of statutory responsibilities, but means by which local people meet their needs and achieve their purposes.

Concern for the value of community responsibility would require an organisational capacity to look beyond problems and needs met by existing services. Problems and issues of concern would not be set by the services provided alone, but would reflect those felt by local people.

Concern for the value of community responsibility can be fulfilled in many ways apart from direct service provision. It involves the activities of other agencies, both public and private, as well as the activities of the local authority. The management of action is matched by the management of influence. A local authority can use its many links with other agencies to influence their decisions.

The local authority can be a facilitator for individuals, local groups and voluntary bodies, helping them achieve their aims in dealing with other agencies, as illustrated by the examples from

Brent and Gloucestershire quoted in Chapter 3. The expertise that the local authority deploys, the intelligence and the information that it stores, can be a resource for other organisations.

Concern for the value of community responsibility could be given expression in a wide variety of ways. The local authority might prepare an annual review representing the council's assessment of the main problems facing its area. The council itself, from being a meeting that merely considers committee business, could become a forum to discuss the report, meeting with public involvement in different parts of the local authority.

Influence can be exercised in many ways. The management of influence is a task for the new management. Strategies can vary from consultation to campaigning. A local authority must know its own resources. Councillors and officers who sit as representatives of the local authority on outside bodies are often unused resources for influence. They could report on their work and seek policy guidance as an element in the management of influence. Local authorities could set up advisory bodies, committees of inquiry or even standing committees on issues of public concern, even where the local authority has no direct responsibility, as some local authorities have set up police committees and health committees.

In an era of constraint, the fragmentation of resources between a multitude of agencies may require an overview through the local authority. A special budgetary presentation would show the use of public funds in an area and be a stimulus to public debate and discussion. The message given to staff and to the public is that to solve a problem or to realise an opportunity the local authority does not have to act directly.

The way a local authority fulfils its community responsibility can take many differing forms. It can involve conflict as well as co-operation, division as well as consensus, campaigning as well as bargaining. The local authority has a choice, if it recognises its responsibilities.

## PUBLIC SERVICE

The new management puts a value on public service. That requires 'a political act of will, that public services should be constructed, so that they serve their consumers needs, not the convenience of those providing them' (National Consumer Council, 1979, p. 21).

The words 'public service' are used so readily that their significance in service for the public is lost. Yet to the new management the words define purposes for local government. Traditional management has valued not service *for* the public but the subtly different service *to* the public. The professional ideal assumes that the public's needs are known with professional authority. The motivation is not service for the public, but a high standard of professional performance. Concern for the value of public service raises the issue of whether a high standard of professional performance is the best public service.

The words need pondering upon. If value is placed on public service, what does it require? It may require new forms of organisation. It requires a weight to be placed on public demands and public reaction to services provided. It means much greater public involvement. It requires concern for the quality of service. This is the emphasis given in Sweden by the Government's service message.

> The work of improving the public's opportunities of actively participating in the re-modelling of society and of creating good contact between individuals and authority is of prime importance. Members of the public as customers have the right to demand quality of service.
>
> (Statens Institute for Personaletveckling (SIPU), 1984)

If local authorities saw public service rather than the provision of services as their primary responsibility, then staff would be expected to seek out their clients' and customers' views. 'Close to the customer' (Peters and Waterman 1980) would be the message. Quality of service would be expected.

Management processes can reflect the value of public service. Local authorities could

> analyse their service, to study their relationship with the public, to identify their customers' needs and to define the basic ideas behind their work and goals.
>
> (SIPU, 1984)

If a local authority placed value on public service, it would seek knowledge of the qualities the public wants in a service. Those qualities are not necessarily those emphasised by the local authority. The techniques developed in Sweden search out these differences.

The first task is to know the services provided. For each service provided the actual and potential customers have to be established. These customers and the providing organisations are both surveyed to establish the relative importance attached to key characteristics of service quality (e.g. speed of service, dealing with complaints, etc.). There can be qualities that customers and service organisations both regard as important. But there can be qualities that customers regard as important and the organisation does not, while some qualities the organisation regards as important will not necessarily be so regarded by the customers. The organisation committed to public service needs to know these differences and to reflect upon them – even if there are good reasons for the difference.

A local authority committed to public service would need to know more about its customers and clients – both present and potential. It would use survey and marketing techniques. It would need to know who its customers were and who were not, and why. A local authority needs to know how it rations its services.

The value of public service leads to an emphasis on complaints, and on learning from them. A local authority could signal its commitment to public service and to quality of service by requiring all complaints to be answered in twenty-four hours. Complaints and suggestions could be encouraged. A Freephone service for complaints and suggestions could be provided. One American local authority 'provides complaints forms in the local newspaper and in the city's monthly newsletter. In addition, a key city official spends two hours one Saturday morning each month at the downtown shopping mall. Either the Mayor or a member of the city council sits at a table in the main concourse of the mall to talk with residents and answer questions'. (Barbour *et al.*, 1984, p. 22).

A local authority committed to the value of public service re-appraises its communications with the public. As in Bradford forms would be reviewed, notices rewritten, pamphlets revised (Whiting, 1983). Material sent to the public should be tested to establish whether it can be understood. From within an organisation, it is hard to understand what is not understood outside. The local authority communicates too through its offices, its doorways and its reception arrangements. They often do not convey a welcome to the public.

The manager can walk the streets of the authority as he can walk the corridors of its offices. Each senior manager could perhaps spend a week each year in the field, join a councillor in his surgery, or sit at reception desks. The manager needs to know the world where public and local authority touch each other.

An American local authority has undertaken a canvass of every household and business to learn their views on the local authority and its services. 'Community canvassing' reflects an emphasis on public service – as well as providing an important development activity for local authority staff (Barbour *et al.*, 1984).

A local authority placing value on public service would ensure that the public understood the service available. Clients of local authority services would be given information on their rights as advocated by a National Council of Voluntary Organisations

Working Party (NCVO, 1984). Social workers would draw up contracts with their clients (Smith, 1985).

Concern for the value of public service can lead to new public involvement in local authority decisions. New possibilities for community polling open up with new technology (Barbour, *et al.*, 1984). Participation could develop from issues, such as structure planning, that are not understood, to issues on the budget that can be. Decision-makers committed to public service need to know at least whether the public seek lower or higher expenditure, and are prepared to pay for it. They need to know the public's differing views on the balance of expenditure between services.

Public involvement can extend to user control of activities. If the aim is public service then user control, subject to whatever financial or policy limits the authority imposes, enables those who use the service to determine its running. That is surely public service.

Concern for the value of public service challenges the existing working of local authorities. For it raises and leaves unanswered the question – who does the existing pattern of activities serve and does the local authority actually know?

## A VALUED STAFF

The new management places value on its staff. Services are provided through staff, often in direct contact with the public. Because quality is determined in direct interaction, the quality of the staff in action determines the quality of the service, and public reaction to the service and perhaps to the local authority. A local authority will never achieve value for money with a devalued staff.

Learning is through staff as well as through councillors. The local authority touches its environment at many points. At any one moment many local authority employees are in contact with the public. Work may not take place in the safety of organisationally defined space, but in the houses and the streets of the authority. Environmental knowledge, and knowledge of problems and responses are held in many heads.

There is a rich potential for initiative amongst the staff of the local authority, whose pattern of working often means that they have to make their decisions far from the safety of an office. Bureaucratic rules never fit reality. The quality of initiative is a resource that can be used, if the local authority values its staff.

The traditional management of local authorities values staff not as staff but as professionals. One consequence is that the authority is seen and felt as placing low value on the non-professional and on low status professionals. The local authority does not employ staff but employs professionals – and others – and manual workers. Division is written into the working of the local authority.

Over-emphasis on professionalism has prevented the develop-ment of a sense of responsibility for staff. A professional is trained to be responsible to the profession not to the authority. Professional autonomy is the ideal. There is an organisational respect for the professional, but no organisational concern for the professional as a member of staff – for morale and motivation, or for development. The profession is assumed to be self-motivated and self-developing.

Concern for value of staff leads to stress on communication with staff, formally and informally. Consultation with the unions is used to the full, but communication with the staff is not restricted to that channel. Staff newspapers, meetings for staff, training courses and informal contacts can ensure staff learn, not merely the policies, but the purposes of the authority. Councillors and senior management should be seen and known to staff.

Concern for the value of staff requires that communication is two-way. The new management seeks to learn from staff about problems encountered in the field, about ideas for policy develop-ment and about public reaction. Short-cuts are made in hierarchies. Discussion groups bring together staff from all levels. In Halton the chief executive regularly meets staff in groups drawn from all grades and levels to discuss the work of the authority. Project groups can bring together field-workers, middle management, senior staff and councillors on particular issues. Departmental conferences can be held for learning and for communicating.

Concern for the value of staff leads to an emphasis on success. Good performance is praised in council and committee. The local authority seeks to build pride in its staff, because it values them.

Staff selection receives emphasis – if staff matter, then their selection matters. Staff training and development become a top priority. The Audit Commission has allocated 3 per cent of its budget to staff training. Policy without a commitment to train and develop staff for that policy is to prove ineffective. The new management implies a new emphasis on management development. All staff have an opportunity to discuss with their superior in the organisation problems and opportunities, failures and success as development and setbacks in their own career. There is a continuing emphasis on and review of the instruments of personnel policy.

Through an active personnel policy, the new management signals the value it places on staff. The new management realise that high performance by the authority depends on staff. Staff will never know that unless they are shown it in many ways and at many times.

# AN ENTREPRENEURIAL APPROACH

The new management values an entrepreneurial approach. Local government has always had its entrepreneurs in councillors and officers who broke through the existing routines of service provision and the accepted traditions to seize new opportunities. They worked against the grain of traditional management.

Traditional management places weight on the existing pattern of services, and on accepted professional practice. The norms of public accountability are interpreted as requiring the avoidance of risk.

In a changing environment innovation and change are required, although more difficult to achieve in an era of constraint.

> The eighties promise to be different for the public manager and in many ways, more difficult and challenging. Resources will not be as readily available as they have been in the past and this circumstance can cause one to naturally hunker down to make a smaller target. It will surprise few that this is not terribly satisfying behaviour. The municipal managers who will stand out in the decade ahead are those who are willing to redefine resources, the community, and their roles very different. They will be those who are willing to take risks, who are imbued with the spirit, knowledge, and skills of the entrepreneur. To these brave souls the eighties belong, and to them the redefinition of public management will fall. Public entrepreneurs be with it.
>
> (Fisher, 1983, p. 14)

This American writer asserts the values of the entrepreneurial approach.

The public entrepreneur is not the private entrepreneur. He uses the entrepreneurial approach in collective endeavour for public service. An entrepreneurial approach cannot be rigidly confined in a definition. In local government it has some of the following characteristics:

- *Searching for opportunities.* The entrepreneurial approach is distinguished by a readiness to look for opportunities, rather than to be overwhelmed by problems and the day-by-day work of service provision.
- *Concern to innovate.* The entrepreneurial approach seeks and uses new ideas.
- *Flexibility in implementation.* The entrepreneurial approach adapts and changes plans and projects in the light of experience.
- *A readiness to take risks.* The entrepreneurial approach is ready to back as yet unproven ideas.

- *Looks outwards for resources.* The entrepreneurial approach is not limited to the resources available within the organisation, but will search the environment for possible sources of funds.
- *Forms links to establish projects.* The entrepreneurial approach is distinguished by a capacity to build links – not least in gathering resources together. Resources available from one source may have to be matched with resources from other sources. Resources in one form (buildings) may have to be matched to resources available in other forms (finance).
- *Creates new organisational forms.* Ventures that bring the local authority into new relationship with external bodies may require the development of organisational structures that differ from established patterns of local government administration.
- *Relaxes traditional control procedures.* The entrepreneurial approach needs a degree of flexibility which may sit uneasily with traditional local government control procedures.

There are dilemmas in the entrepreneurial approach. Opportunities realised by such an approach can distort the priorities of an authority's programme. An entrepreneurial approach can then frustrate political purpose. What is required is an entrepreneurial approach guided by political purpose.

## CONCLUSION

Organisational values distinguish the new management from traditional management:

- The new management stresses the role of local authorities as local government rather than merely the provision of services.
- The new management supports rather than limits the political process.
- The new management is based on the authority's concern for the local community, and is not limited to the services provided.
- The new management aims at service for the public, rather than service to the public.
- The new management focuses on staff as the means of learning, and of change, and cannot neglect their development.
- The new management creates and seizes opportunities to achieve political purpose and is not limited by the routines of past practices.

The values are easily stated, but less easily achieved. Existing procedures, structures and staffing policies are grounded in traditional management. New procedures, structures and staffing policies are required for the new management.

# Part One – Conclusion

The traditional management of local authorities is geared to the maintenance of the activities necessary to the existing pattern of service provision. Local authorities are by no means unique in that. In most organisations the routines of the day-by-day work absorb much and, indeed in some cases, all of the attention of management. The short-term urgency of immediate demands can drive out concern for longer-term direction. What has to be done now has an imperative that leaves no time for concern with what might be. The necessities of service provision can absorb managerial effort to the neglect of change in the activities of the organisation.

Traditional management reinforced the organisational tendency for an operational perspective. The committee system has focused political attention on existing activities. The organising principles of bureaucracy are the principles necessary for the continuities of service provision. Professionalism supports the maintenance of present standards and the performance of tasks in prescribed ways. Traditional management has assumed that existing activities could and should continue relatively unchanged and unchanging.

The new local management of local authorities cannot make that assumption. As management for local government, it must be concerned both with changing and with choice.

Local government in a changing environment requires a local authority to respond to change with change. Present activities cannot be assumed to be adequate to the problems and opportunities of a changed and changing environment. As local government, local authorities need a capacity for responsive change.

Local government requires more than responsive change. The political process can be a means of responsive change, but it is also a means of directive change, expressing local choice.

> Responsive change is about the maintenance of the existing pattern of society in changed circumstance. Directed change is about changing that pattern.
>
> (Stewart, 1983)

As local government, local authorities need a capacity for directive change.

The new management supports the role of local authorities as local government. It builds a capacity both for responsive change and for directive change. This requires procedures for:

- learning of the changing environment and of the impact of the authority on that environment (Chapter 5);
- challenging existing policies and choice on future policies (Chapter 6);
- choice in setting direction (Chapter 7);
- leaving space in implementation for responsiveness (Chapter 8).

These procedures require support in the organisational structure of the authority (Chapter 9) and in its staffing policies and processes (Chapter 10).

While a local authority responds and changes, chooses and directs as local government, it will have to maintain many of its existing activities as a provider of services. As a provider of services, the local authority still requires many of the strengths of traditional management, maintaining standards of service and reliability of provision. The problem is not to replace traditional management's strength in supporting service provision, but to overcome its weakness for local government.

What is written in Part Two is about building countervailing forces in the organisational framework. Support for the role of local authorities as local government has to be given by appropriate procedures, structures and staffing policies. That role requires special protection in local authorities, both because traditional management is deeply ingrained in the working of the local authority and because the routines of service provision necessarily and rightly will continue to occupy the main attention of most of the staff of local authorities. Building the new management has to be carried out in and through organisations that have been formed by traditional management and that will continue to require many of its characteristics. It is not sufficient to outline the changes required. The changes must be grounded in organisational understanding and sustained by continuing organisational management. Those themes provide the conclusion (Chapter 11) of Part Two of this book.

# PART TWO

# The Search for the New Management

# 5

# The Learning Local
# Authority

## NO NEW MANAGEMENT WITHOUT NEW
## LEARNING

The new management builds a learning local authority. Traditional
management's need for learning is limited by concentration on the
established pattern of service provision. It assumes that the services
are required, and have to be provided, which is the main task for
management. Learning is restricted by the requirements of the
established services.

The new management is active, exploring the need for change.
There can be change in the services provided or in the ways they are
provided. There can be change in action or in influence. There can be
change in the organisation and its working. All or any of such
changes may be considered necessary for local government. It is a
matter for local choice, but the choice will be related to local
circumstance. That implies an understanding of the environment, of
the impact of existing services and of the working of the organisation. Understanding comes from learning established on a continuing basis, for what is learnt at one moment may later have to be
unlearnt. Neither environment nor organisation stands still merely
because learning has stood still.

Learning, and the monitoring necessary to learning, is presented
as the start of the policy process, although it is customary to present
monitoring as the culmination of the policy process. Policy is made
and then monitored. But local authorities do not make policy afresh.
They are already carrying out a wide range of policies, which if not
explicit are implicit in the services provided. Those services are being
provided and have an impact on the environment. The environment
itself is changing. The starting point is learning about the present in
order to determine what should or should not be changed. Change

does not follow automatically from learning; choice is involved. Choice requires learning about the present, otherwise it is choice in the abstract, unrelated to present reality.

Learning can lead to the challenging of present activities or of the present organisation, and to the possibility of change. Without the possibility of change, there is no point in learning.

## ORGANISATIONAL BARRIERS TO LEARNING

There are major barriers to learning in any organisation. Organisations maintain areas of relative stability in a world of change. The organisational framework, through its structures, its procedures and its processes of socialisation, provides protection to that area of stability. Organisations are organised to carry out certain activities in certain ways. Organisations can be organised for change, but of a type planned or predicted. One does not organise for total instability or prepare for total change. Organisation imposes its own regularities.

The organisational framework protects those regularities. The way work is divided up between departments or into tiers, the procedures routinising the way work is performed, and the processes of socialisation, all help to establish and to reproduce those regularities.

An organisation learns, but it learns what it is organised to learn. Organisational frameworks protect and have to protect against indiscriminate learning. The boundaries of the organisation have to be protected, so that tasks may be performed. Those boundaries protect it against learning which is seen as irrelevant. Paradoxically it can mean the organisation only learns what it already knows. From the apparently irrelevant the organisation can learn the unexpected. Yet the very fact of organisation tends to exclude the unexpected. Organisations can counter this tendency by allowing an element of 'disorganisation'. The unexpected and the unplanned can be allowed across organisational boundaries – at least occasionally.

Organisational tendencies to restrict learning are reinforced in the traditional management of local government. Professionalism is a powerful force restricting learning to established professional patterns. Local authorities do not easily hear of, or accept, information or knowledge that challenges accepted professional knowledge or practice.

The organising principles of local government reinforce unlearning. The functional principles cannot encompass learning that falls between the functional divides. The principles of uniformity eliminate the learning that comes from diversity. The principle of hierarchy sets barriers to learning in the tiers that separate the centre of the local authority from its periphery, each tier sifting out the uncomfortable unfitting information from which learning derives.

The local authority has in the political process, a source of learning that need not be restricted to present organisational concerns. In traditional management, however, the political process is often restricted by the committee system to the regularities of service provision.

## COMMUNICATIONS ACROSS THE BOUNDARIES

Learning about the environment depends upon information flowing into the authority. There is the information that comes from requests, demands, pressure and protest. There is information systematically collected for the day-by-day management of services. Channels across local authority boundaries carry their own bias. Awareness of this bias is a first step in learning. Demand for existing services is not by itself an indication that those services should continue to be provided, rather than a service not currently provided for which there is much less expressed demand. If a local authority concentrates on domiciliary care for the elderly, rather than care in the community, it will by that policy condition demand. Demand will focus on the service available. From a housing waiting list one learns about demand for the housing that is available. One learns nothing about the social problems that may underlie the demand and little about the potential demand for housing that is not, but could be made, available. Channels structured around existing provision of the services are not by themselves adequate for the new management. They have to be supplemented by channels free of the bias of existing provision.

Apart from such a system bias, there can be a bias due to varying access. Access to the local authority is not equally open to all. Access is limited in a variety of ways, and those limits create a bias in communication channels.

Access to a particular service may require knowledge of the service, of what authority provides it and of the procedures for obtaining it. Knowledge of the services available is not perfectly or evenly distributed. Even services or benefits freely available for all are not taken up without special efforts. Welfare rights campaigns increase the take-up of benefits to which people are entitled.

The policy adopted by the authority can itself distort demand. Research into one authority's administration of housing improvement grant concluded that the 'service *in effect* discriminated against inner areas' (Webster *et al.*, p. 178). The researchers argued:

> This was primarily due to lack of demand from those areas. Demand was expressed at four separate points in the application process, in an initial inquiry, in the decision to proceed to obtaining application forms, in the submission of the application and in completing the necessary paperwork for the final decision to be taken. A variety of factors are likely to affect take-up and some of them such as income and tenure cannot be directly controlled by the local authority. However, the laissez-faire attitude towards housing improvement, reflected in the level of promotion, area improvement and compulsory improvement will not have encouraged improvement activity. Moreover, our view is that the local authority's policy of achieving comprehensive improvement and a high standard of repairs has actively discouraged applicants from proceeding, although it must be pointed out that this effect would have been greatly exacerbated by the fact that nationally defined levels of eligible expenses remained static while building costs increased sharply.
>
> (Webster *et al.*, n.d. p. 178)

Underlying the rigorous standards was 'a shared professional view' that 'to be worthwhile and to justify the spending of public money, the property should be brought up to a very good standard to ensure a reasonable life'. This policy supported by the Environmental Committee 'may unintentionally have discouraged legitimate improvement activity and appears to conflict with the aim of improving the living conditions of those who occupy the worst properties, in particular the residents of inner areas' (Webster *et al.*, n.d., pp. 178–79).

Bargaining power can affect the readiness to listen, to learn and to respond.

> This bargaining power can help to persuade professionals to review priorities and to ease routines. Any individual householder applying to the local Planning Department for permission to convert or extend a building usually finds that the application has to be tailored very carefully to fit the planning *regime* that has been laid down within that particular planning department. The regimes vary a little from one authority to another but they are all designed to help junior and middle-management planning staff to

do a routine job and deal fairly with every individual. To use much discretion might look like favouritism.

When the large-scale developer seeks planning permission it is different. A package of planning permissions can be put together with both sides talking things over at top level and reaching a compromise that fulfils basic planning requirements but relates them to the needs and the style of the scheme as a whole.

(Gibson, 1984, p. 80)

The distance to local authority offices can deny access to the many with transport difficulties. The offices themselves do not always make access easy. The entrance to a town hall, built to celebrate the pride of the Victorian entrepreneur, is not inviting to all. Buildings can deter the uncertain and the inexperienced. Forms, letters and notices can add to rather than allay confusion.

A perceptive analysis of public relations for Warwickshire County Council said:

... many of those consulted recognised the awesome obstacles that the steps at Shire Hall may present to many of the population who would find a journey into the dark reception area to be greeted by a uniformed, albeit pleasant, custodian, a daunting prospect.

There is a tendency in all County offices to barricade reception staff behind sliding screens through which contact is made by a bell or a knock. The client remains cut off and his access to the hallowed ground beyond is controlled by a sliding screen which has all the charity of a guillotine.

(Warwickshire County Council, 1982, p. 7)

There are many who guard access to the services of the local authority. The receptionist at the desk, the social work assistant assessing the need for aids for the handicapped or the housing assistant handling a housing application can all deny access to a service, redirect to other parts of the organisation, or transform a request for one service into a demand for another.

One of the many elements which may affect decisions about who receives what services is the person who looks after the telephone or sits behind the reception desk.

(Hall, 1975, p. 139)

In short, reception staff acted as a powerful 'buffer' between field workers and their clients and potential clients and as such exerted a considerable influence on the provision of primary agency services. Far from performing only a passive function within the organisation, receptionists were frequently operating very much in the area of professional judgement and discretion.

(Hall, 1975, p. 128)

Whether a child problem is treated as the concern of education, social services or the police (or is an issue for the authority at all) can depend on the receptionist.

A local authority has to ration its services. Given scarce resources, rationing is inevitable. Council and committee set the limits for rationing services when they determine budgetary allocations, but they do not necessarily determine how the rationing will be carried out, i.e. how the demand for the service is to be satisfied with the resources available.

It would, in principle, be possible for council and committee to go further and determine how each service should be allocated in relation to potential demand. Rationing could then be carried out according to clear criteria, determined by the local authority, with only the minimal discretion inevitable in any administrative act. A points scheme for the allocation of housing is rationing openly recognised and settled in committee discussion and debate.

For some services such rationing can be over-rigid, inhibiting responsiveness by those closer to the demand for the service. It may prove impossible to predetermine criteria for varying demand. There are political costs involved. An authority that determines criteria for a service acknowledges a failure to meet potential demand for a service. Such acknowledgement is not readily made.

Rationing may take place outside the control of the local authority. Rationing is carried out by public ignorance and by distance, by reluctance to challenge officialdom in its fortresses, and by field-workers fitting services to limited resources.

Channels of communication based on service provision, reflect the bias that comes from rationing, whether it is the rationing planned by the authority, administered by field-workers, or the rationing of variable public response. Those channels of communication will not adequately convey demands that did not surface or were rejected. To understand the bias, the local authority has to understand how its services are rationed and with what impact – essential learning for management. Each year every committee could break out of the constraints of its routine agendas to consider the issue of how the services for which they are responsible are rationed. If the answer is not known, then there is a need for learning.

## COMMUNICATION WITHIN

Much information is present in local authorities. Each field-worker is a potential source of information. The local authority touches the environment at many points and in these contacts learning takes place, but it often remains with the field-worker, remote from senior management.

The hierarchies of the local authority are the formal channels of communiction between field and centre. Down those hierarchies flows information on decisions and action required. Up those hierarchies flows information on action taken and problems encountered. These channels of communication have their own distortions. As policies are translated into implementable action, misunderstanding occurs. At the centre necessary background information fails to be understood.

Information does not easily mount hierarchies. It has to be sifted and reduced in its diversity. Abstracting conclusions from many cases, grouping disparate information into broad categories and eliminating information that does not 'fit' becomes the task of middle management. This process can reduce learning, because it reduces the unfamiliar or the unexpected to the categories traditionally expected by the organisation. There is a bias in hierarchical channels of communication that has to be understood by a learning local authority. The bias reduces non-conformity to conformity.

The bias as found in hierarchical channels of communication reinforces the barriers set at organisational boundaries because they both reject non-conforming information. If the present practice of the authority discriminates against certain groups, that discrimination will also be present in the communication channel. If institutional racism is

> a description of policies, practices, structures, procedures, rules and regulations, which have developed over time and are embedded in the customs and practices of the institution,
>
> (Ouseley, 1984, p. 139)

then the channels of communications will be conditioned by the institutional racism and learning of the consequences will be barred, unless new channels can be constructed and listened to.

The need is to learn about how the authority learns, but even more, about how it does not learn.

## USING THE INFORMATION WITHIN

The starting point, because it is so readily available, is the information available to staff and to councillors. Each is a rich source of ideas and impressions. Each sees much more that is relevant to the authority than is ever recorded.

The problem is not the availability of information, but how to use it. The variety of such information means it cannot be reduced to routines without destroying its value. The local authority will only be able to use this information by creating new channels down which such information will flow, and by signalling to its staff its wide interest in information about its services and their impact, and about problems and opportunities faced.

The views and ideas of staff have to be actively sought. Hierarchies have to be by-passed in staff meetings, group discussions and seminars. Individual members of staff have to be given opportunities to discuss both their work and views.

Staff can be encouraged to note any problem or issue they consider the authority should be dealing with. The windshield techniques developed by the Urban Institute for 'supervisors and managers driving around town' can be extended as it has been in Redwood City in California, which 'has a simple data service request form that city employees can use to report problems such as pot holes, down tree limbs, malfunctioning street lights, unsightly public facilities, etc. The form is signed by the employee and is routed directly to the department in charge. The reporting employee is also notified about what action will be taken' (Barbour *et al.*, 1984, p. 19). Those who walk the streets of the local authority see much, but record little, beyond the limits defined for their role. An environmental health officer records environmental health problems, whereas a social worker records social problems, but both are seeing other problems that can go unrecorded.

Complaints are little used as sources of information, beyond the immediate response. The local authority can analyse complaints by subject or by organisation, by geography or over time, to establish patterns which show symptoms of relative discontent. Patterns of usage of council facilities are an important guide, non-usage being as important an indicator as usage. Why are some libraries more used than others?

The councillor – and particularly the councillor deeply concerned with a local area – is an under-utilised resource; the surgery, the letters received, the telephone calls and the endless contacts form impressions which lack any means of expression in those local authorities in which the service committee is the only formal setting of the council. A service-based organisation has difficulty using information that does not fit service boundaries. It transforms all information into service information, eliminating learning that the information makes possible.

## OPENING UP THE AUTHORITY TO LEARNING

The local authority needs new channels of communication across its boundaries if it is to improve learning. There are many possible channels of communication; each has its own strengths and its own distortions; each can complement the other. Many channels are needed.

Survey techniques can be developed. Cleveland County Council has, since reorganisation, carried out a citizen's survey to indicate the degree of satisfaction with particular services, gaining the ability to analyse changing attitudes over time (Mobbs, 1985). Social surveys and market research are important instruments for learning. Because local authorities are not in a market, it becomes more not less important to carry out survey work. Richmond London Borough commissioned Market and Opinion Research International (MORI) to carry out a study of residents attitudes to rates and services. Its main aims were:

- to measure overall attitudes to Richmond Council, with particular reference to its allocation of financial resources;
- to gauge usage of and satisfaction with a range of Council services;
- to examine priorities between different service areas;
- to establish residents' attitudes to the options facing the Council over the trade-off between the level of rate increase and the maintaining of council services in Richmond;
- to evaluate communications with and from the council and its image in dealing with residents;
- to measure attitudes to certain central government policies relating to local government;
- to determine variations in attitudes between different groups of residents.

(MORI, 1985)

In Halton a number of steps have been taken to open up new channels of communication. In the Stewards Avenue Refurbishment Project architectural and design staff and quantity surveying staff were located in a converted house on the estate. The architects worked directly from the estate and were thus acceptable for tenants.

A major lesson was learned within the organisation. It was a traumatic experience for professional architectural and quantity surveying staff to work from a council house in an estate such as this. They found themselves not employed as designers but as negotiators, community workers, handymen, community policemen, and many other roles. They also learned that they actually had to make decisions, and that quite trivial and mundane and ordinary assessments, were important to people, and that successful management is about activity at this level.

(Turton, 1984)

The councillor is a source of learning that is often insufficiently used by the authority. The councillors surgery can be a learning centre for the authority willing and able to use it. In Nottinghamshire, work is being undertaken to monitor council surgery work and to see how it may be supported as 'part of a wider study in the context of community development work about channels of communication between communities and their local authority ...' (Richardson, 1985, p. 36).

User discussion groups can be an important learning process. The small group of children, or of parents, or of old people, or of all, called together to discuss how parks could be improved, is important to learning. Old people can discuss the running of old peoples homes, library users discuss book selection; there are rich seams of learning to be mined. In Camden, as part of the development of care for the under 5s, there were held 'a (long) series of twenty-two group discussions with various categories of parents, and with professionals involved with the referral process. The groups were recruited by a professional recruiter, took place either in a domestic setting (someone's lounge) or a community hall, contained an average six or seven parents and a researcher, were taped, and lasted one and a half to two hours ...' (Heiser, 1985, p. 84).

New forms of public involvement lead to direct learning in the provision of services. In housing estates run by tenant co-operatives, the tenants' experiences and responses become part of effective management. A Department of the Environment study of management co-operatives in local authority housing said:

We have described in some detail the two co-operative arrangements for repair and maintenance, cleaning and caretaking, and their emphasis on making improvements to the dwellings and the estate. While these provide obvious advantages to the tenants, it is also clear that the local authority's stock of dwellings under co-operative management are being well cared for. The co-operative appeared to provide a better standard of day-to-day repair and maintenance as small problems were attended to quickly and efficiently and all the co-operatives carefully planned for larger scale repairs and cyclical maintenance.

(Department of the Environment, 1982, p. 42)

Direct public involvement can lead to learning for the public as well as for the authority.

When Stockport Social Services Department decided to give physically handicapped people, the parents of mentally handicapped, and elderly people a decisive say in how their clubs and centres were run and how their budgets were spent, the initial decisions were different from those that would have been made by the authority. Chairs, tables and curtains were bought, for example, which were not what the authority would have purchased. Experience here also suggests that, in managing, clients initially may act conservatively, making choices on the basis of the experience of a powerless past. A more developed model is found in a day centre in Islington where mentally handicapped centre users help to interview and select staff.

(NCVO, 1985)

Where the local authority provides a choice to its customers or clients, the authority can learn from the choices made. The use of fees and charges can test demand for a service, as the increase in charges for school meals has done. Parental choice on schools is in effect a channel of communication on parental views. Choice can be extended. Some social service departments have issued books of tickets to give choice to the parents of mentally handicapped children.

Combinations of values can be traded in for varying periods of different forms of care for their child – evening baby-sitting, a shopping creche facility, overnight, week-end or holiday respite in a home or with foster-parents.

(Smith, 1985, pp. 79–80)

From choices made the authority learns to adapt service provision.

Each channel carries its own distortion. Choice can be distorted by variation in resources, whether it be in the resources of knowledge and know-how, or in financial resources. Forms of public involvement can be distorted by the articulate and by the manipulators. Surveys can be distorted by their own artificiality. User groups can be distorted by their setting.

Response lies in the creation of many channels of communication. The truth lies not in one, but in many, for there is not likely to be one interest, but many; not one viewpoint, but many viewpoints. Channels of communication must be capable of diversity.

There is a limit to the number of channels of communication that can be handled by a local authority. Channels of communication that are not responded to silt up with ineffectiveness. The local authority cannot, therefore, endlessly multiply channels of communication to overcome distortion. Nor would such multiplication by itself overcome the biases that lie within channels or in organisational responses.

A local authority can only overcome such problems by awareness of the bias in its learning and by concentrating on building countervailing channels to correct that bias. Much that has been written above focuses on correcting the bias towards the reinforcement of the existing pattern of service provision. There is likely to be a bias in communication channels against the deprived in our society who suffer in communication.

Roger Jefferies, an experienced chief executive, has advised the form of letter which those who seek action from a local authority should write:

Chief Executive
Town Hall, Bridgetown

Dear Sir
Open Space Behind Cross Street:<br>Boundary Fence

---

Would you please direct this letter to the correct department or let me know some information of the following matters:

a)   The responsibility for the repair of the fence at the boundary of my property with the land behind Cross Street owned by the council;

b)   what steps the council is taking to prevent rubbish being tipped on the site, and whether the present mess will be cleared up;

c)   what plans the council has for the future of the site?

The condition of the site is an eyesore, and needs early attention. There are rumours that the council proposes to sell the site for factory development. Can you tell me when this was considered by the council and where may I read the minutes or a report?

I would like your officers to visit the site to see the fence and can be available in the week beginning 1 September, at any time during the day, if they will let me know beforehand.

Yours faithfully<br>(Jefferies, 1982, p. 45)

Roger Jefferies has correctly set out the language of organisational acceptability, but that language is a foreign language for many. The public outside the organisation may speak a different language from those within.

Take two people's attitudes to the words NOW, SOON and LATER. A local housewife is concerned about toddlers running off the pavement at a dangerous traffic intersection. She wants traffic railings or a pelican crossing, *now*, or very *soon*. She goes to see a conscientious local government planner who agrees with her the matter is urgent. It ought to be investigated, correlated with other traffic problems, checked with the regional highways people, set down as a committee paper, negotiated through the first round at committees, adjusted to accommodate cutbacks, re-submitted to catch the budget allocation for the next fiscal year. With everyone doing his bit there's an excellent prospect that the thing will be done if not *now*, at least very *soon* – say within twelve to eighteen months. The mum with the toddler wonders whether they are talking the same language.

(Gibson, 1984, p. 108)

The local authority that seeks to learn must be aware of that potential for distortion and build positive discrimination in channels of communication. Those whose voices are not heard in those channels can be sought out in new ways.

The new management need the experience of working in deprived areas to build up awareness of non-learning as part of staff development for senior management. The experience of action centres, the reading (after, if necessary, the translation) of the grassroots press, the knowledge of community workers, can all be used. The differing experiences of race relations committees and women's committees, each seeking channels of communications for learning what the local authority has not previously been able to learn, have shown the possibility of breaking out of past stereotypes of communication.

Women's committees have thus been exploring new structures and ways of meeting that overcome the barriers women face. Open meetings, working groups, public meetings and co-options have all been attempts to bring women into the policy-making process. There has been an emphasis on informality, collective working and attempts to break down local authority hierarchies. Publicity has been carefully designed to reach and be understood by local women, and leaflets, day events, exhibitions, women's buses, and so on, have been experiments in reaching women that are not in organised groups.

(Goss, 1984, p. 117)

All these approaches have their own distortion, but the distortion is not that of existing channels of communication and that is their value. These channels provide a countervailing source of learning. To provide new channels does not necessarily guarantee their use. Nor does it guarantee that what is learnt will be attended to. Learning has to be evaluated and evaluation for local government is a political act. What is argued for is not a particular result from learning, but a greater capacity for learning.

A capacity for learning will not be achieved by an authority that defends its own information. Open government is a necessary part of the learning local authority because it declares an openness to learning. This goes beyond the past practices and beyond the formal implementation of the Local Government (Access to Information) Act (1985). A commitment to open government as part of the learning local authority invites the involvement that is learning.

Steps have been taken in Brent to open up council and committee to the public, by giving the public a period at each meeting to ask questions. In Cheshire this practice has been adopted for committees. An even more important step would be new forms of council meetings which focused not on the business of particular committees and on the running of the council, but provided a forum for public debate on the problems and opportunities facing the area.

Change to a learning local authority will not be easily achieved. Established practices are being challenged, and those practices may be defended by existing organisational interests. Trade unions may be amongst those who resist change. Staff are being asked to change their ways of working and that can be seen as a threat. Experience in local authorities that have moved towards new forms of decentralisation on other modes of working have found that such change may be resisted by the trade unions as imposing new burdens on staff.

Yet change and changing are possible given care. Change to a learning authority realises the full potential of staff. It expresses the value placed on staff from whom or through whom learning derives. Yet staff and their unions can come to welcome and have welcomed such changes, provided there is care in preparation, in consultation and, where required, in negotiation. A learning local authority has to be sustained by the staff policies discussed in Chapter 10.


## THE POLITICS OF LEARNING

The learning local authority opens itself to channels of communication, and to the demands and the pressures released. It opens itself, therefore, to the pressure of disappointed demand and to more active politics – whether the growing politics of local pressure groups or the intensification of local party politics. An active politics should be seen as central to authority learning, both as providing information and evaluating it.

A local authority learns through an active complex of pressure groups. Chambers of commerce, voluntary groups, tenants associations and groups representative of ethnic minorities are part of the politics of learning. Groups that rise and fall as issues rise and fall express immediate passions and concerns. A learning local authority can listen to many groups or interests, for each provide information and can be part of the pressure which in a political system provides the basis for evaluation.

The political parties, as well as the political groups on the council, are a direct channel of communication that is not necessarily confined to the existing pattern of service provision. The political process responds more readily to emerging problems and issues than the bureaucratic mode or even than professionalism. There are now far more black councillors than there are black senior officers. It is largely through the political process that authorities have come to focus on such issues as equal opportunities or economic development.

Politics is a means of learning, but is also the basis of evaluation of the learning. 'Voice' in the public sector is the alternative to 'exit' in the market place (Hirschman, 1970). Voice as protest and pressure, demand and complaint gives politics its information. Politics carries its own evaluation of the voices, reflecting the differing values of different parties on which the electorate must make their judgement. Debate and discussion by the parties inform that judgement. The long years of party debate on comprehensive education informed public views, while in the enclosed world of the health service the district general hospital was introduced without public debate. Party activity is critical to learning and the interpretation of what is learnt.

The new management recognises the parties as important to the working of local government. Parties can be assisted by the new management, where such assistance is sought. Manifestos can be strengthened by information provided by management. Debates and discussions within all parties can be assisted by access to officer information. The more effective the parties, the more effective the local political process. An informed political process is necessary to effective learning in local government as a political institution.

## OPENING UP THE AUTHORITY TO THE KNOWLEDGE BEYOND

For learning, local authorities require not merely information drawn from their own area, but access to knowledge as it develops beyond their area. Local authorities require the knowledge of how problems are changing in society generally, of the approaches being developed to deal with them, of studies undertaken and of theories built.

As there are channels along which data and information from the community flows so there are channels along which knowledge flows to an authority. As with the channels of communication, so are the channels of knowledge determined by the existing pattern of service provision.

Knowledge flows along professional lines. In professional journals or through professional associations, local government officers learn readily of new and developing knowledge. An engineer will learn about new materials and an environmental health officer will learn about new knowledge on disease. They do not learn so readily about knowledge that lies outside the professional field. Knowledge of the social consequences of design, or the economics of environmental health, does not always flow along professional channels.

Professionalism is a valuable source of changing knowledge, but for knowledge channels to be dominated by professionalism is a barrier to knowledge that challenges professionalism. Nor is there any channel for knowledge about fields in which there is no established professional base in local government.

A learning local authority needs new channels for knowledge. The political process needs direct support by knowledge not dependent on professional sources alone. At present councillors in most local authorities have no established access to channels of knowledge beyond that available in departments, although some local authorities have appointed political advisers or research assistants to provide new channels to knowledge.

Close to a local authority there will be knowledge centres such as universities, polytechnics and colleges of further education on which local authorities can draw. Some are funded directly by local authorities, yet are little used as resources for knowledge and research. A learning local authority will seek new links with such centres, offering access to students and facilities for research, and seeking to establish forms of working which will draw in staff for advice and consultation. Academics can be used as advisers to working groups and placed on appropriate advisory committees.

Local authorities made too little use of resources for knowledge, under their own control.

Public libraries like all sectors of local government have to make choices about the allocation of resources to this aspect of the service or that, but there is little evidence to show that local government information was ever seriously considered except by a few more forward looking public libraries.

One reason behind this apparently inexplicable failure to take notice of the information needs of its parent organisation is the independent stance of public libraries which are in local government but not really of it.

(Grayson, 1978, p. 48)

The library service could provide new channels for knowledge to flow into the local authority.

A learning local authority should monitor its channels of knowledge and analyse the bias in those channels. The local authority would identify knowledge sources – e.g. journals and institutions – it could draw upon to correct the bias. A local authority should ensure that some of its staff do not only go to their own professional conferences, but to conferences likely to produce unexpected knowledge.

Channels of knowledge should provide learning that challenges as well as reinforces present practice.

## PLOTTING THE CHANGING ENVIRONMENT

The local authority has not merely to collect information. Information does not turn unchanged into recommendations for action or for inaction. It has to be analysed to identify the significant in the present and in the future. Learning comes from analysis.

Much analysis already takes place in the departments of local government. The work of service provision requires such analysis. The education department needs and uses projections of school populations. The social services department needs information about the number and the conditions of the elderly. The engineers departments uses data on traffic patterns. Departments need data on the present and projections for the future.

This analysis reinforces existing patterns of service provision. For analysis is not a neutral act; judgement is being made about which information is relevant and how it should be arranged. That judgement reflects and reinforces existing organisational assumptions and values. The analysis of data is both a product of evaluation and an evaluation in itself. Analysis by and for traditional management reflects the values embedded in existing patterns of service provision.

The learning required by the new management cannot be so restricted. Plotting the changing environment cannot be restricted to data relevant to existing patterns of service provision. It must be capable of reflecting the learning from new channels of communication and of knowledge. Much of the learning is the softer information of complaint and demand, protest and pressure. Such information suggest symptoms of concern of which analysis must deepen understanding.

Understanding is required of the present and of the future that is contained in the present. Trend analysis is insufficient. Traditional management has used trend analysis because it has assumed continuity. The environment remains unchanged, save by growth; existing needs and problems continue, only they will grow in scale. Trend analysis justifies existing activities.

A trend carried on over time can breed its own reaction. Pendulums, having swung so far, swing back. A political movement to the right carried too far leads to a reaction to the left, and vice versa. If new technology leads to a trend to home-based work, there may be a new trend to seek social contact in leisure. A trend may be broken by a significant event – as the rise in oil prices in the 1970s broke, or symbolised the break, in past trends. Ideas can transform, as ideas on equal opportunities transform perceptions and make relevant the previously irrelevant. The dilemma is not to detect the trend but to detect the break in the trend, and the new direction.

To detect a changing trend is not an easy task, and there are no certain methods. The main requirement is to be aware of the possibility either that a trend carried too far will cause a counter trend or that a new event or a new idea may cause a change in direction. The correct stance towards trend analysis is healthy scepticism enforced by such questions as:

- Is this trend likely to cause a reaction?
- Are there any signs of that reaction?
- What new development can break trends?
- What current event, book, article or broadcast might be a sign of such a break point?

To these questions there are no clear answers, but their asking may give indications. Analysis of emerging problems and issues is not for statisticians alone. It calls for insight and that comes from many disciplines – not excluding that of statisticians, of course!

If plotting the changing environment is to lead to significant learning, it must break away from merely plotting the past into the present and the future. Analysis must be based on different principles than those required for the management of existing services.

# THE EXAMPLE OF BRADFORD

*The Changing Face of Bradford*, published by the Bradford District Council in 1984, provides an example of learning in analysis by reflection rather than a mere analysis of trends (although oddly it is described as such). It is in practice an analysis of an area 'in the grip of a fundamental and profound change – in its economy, its social structures and its environment' (p. 7). It does not cover all the issues affecting the district, but claims to identify some 'of the most important trends and problems which will confront the Council in the next decade' (p. 7). *The Changing Face of Bradford* is not structured according to the services or departments of the local authority, but according to the structure of problems and issues identified:

- Who governs Bradford
- The local economy
- Women's equality
- Race relations
- People, environment and housing
- Poverty, health and welfare
- New technology

Nor is the document limited to the normally accepted organisational boundaries of the District Council. It is concerned with problems facing Bradford, wherever responsibility for dealing with those problems may or may not lie. The document reflects key value choices rather than hides them.

At a time when the Council's own resources are shrinking, it will become more pressing to decide between a more commercial and a 'social support' approach to providing services – and between different demands from different groups for those same resources.

Below are a series of quotations setting out the conclusions following analysis which give the flavour of *The Changing Face of Bradford*:

The council may still be able to make effective decisions in a climate of dwindling resources, but it will need genuinely to share power and responsibility.

(pp. 14–15)

Whilst no-one in the District is immune from the effects of economic decline, the seriousness of the recession must seem very different viewed from say Sloan Square, Canterbury Estate or Little Horton, than say from Bingley, Ilkley or Cullingworth. The danger is that many areas of the District may become permanent unemployment blackspots.

(p. 27)

Many people believe equal opportunities are available. In practice, this depends upon women adopting male methods and fitting in with systems devised by men, with male needs in mind. It means they have to work extra hard along the way.

(p. 36)

In 1983 in West Yorkshire, 59% of all women who worked earned less than £100, compared to just 15% of men.

(p. 39)

Equality of housing means equality of access. If the council wishes to achieve it, perhaps it should question whether the housing needs of black families are seen as a set of inconvenient, special demands, or as the legitimate right of some Bradford citizens.

(p. 58)

The population pressure on our inner city areas shows every sign of increasing. As it increases, the conflicts of demand for space will also increase. Yet paradoxically, despite the demand for land, parts of the inner city are quite derelict.

(p. 67)

The image of the inner city areas as the only badly-off areas in the District has always been a myth. Apart, perhaps, from the quality of the housing council estates have lacked resources at least as much as inner city areas.

(p. 82)

A cause for concern, though, is those children who have no computers at home. Will this widen the educational gap between children from poor homes and those from better-off homes.

(p. 97)

This was a document for learning and so it was seen by the three leaders who, in a hung authority, joined in the Foreword to say:

In broad terms the predictions ... appear to us to be fairly accurate. No doubt there will be disagreement over interpretations and details – and there will be strong political debate about how some of the issues should be tackled.

(Bradford, 1984, p. 3.)

## A PAUSE FOR LEARNING

The learning local authority learns about how it learns, opens up new channels of communication and knowledge both across and within organisational boundaries, opens up new knowledge channels and maps out its understanding.

Organisational learning can over time affect the working of the local authority. A culture of learning can become part of management, if supported by senior management. It would, however, be only too easy for learning to take place but yet not to influence the activities of the local authority. The routines of service provision have their own necessities. Learning can take place but still not influence action. Complaints are analysed; discussions between field-workers and chief officers develop; user groups are formed; maps of community problems are produced; but little happens and in the end learning dries up, for there is little point in learning if action does not follow.

There have to be procedures that will counter the procedures of traditional management, to enforce not so much the learning but reflection on learning with a view to action. Counterveiling procedures must force the organisation to pause in the routines necessary to service provision.

Each year, each unit, each department and each committee, officer and councillor alike, can take organisational time and space to reflect on their learning both about their areas of concern and beyond:

- How successful has the authority been?
- Are we providing good service for the public, and how do we know?
- What failures do we know about and what failures do we suspect?
- What are the public's attitudes to the authority and are they changing, and why?
- How is the authority rationing its services?
- How far does the public's attitude vary, and why?
- What problems and issues are over-emphasised, and which relevant problems and issues neglected?
- Whom does the authority serve, and who is excluded?
- What is changing in the environment of concern, and how will it affect the role of the authority?
- What is changing in the environment of knowledge and how will it affect the authority?
- What should be done?

If these questions are asked of each area of concern they must also be asked more widely by the policy and resources committee, the council, the chief executive and the management team. Learning has to express the community responsibility of local government.

Less important than the particular question is the pause and the questioning. In the end learning has to become part of the authority – and for that it has to be written into the timetabled imperatives of procedures.

## THERE SHOULD BE NO CONCLUSION TO LEARNING

A learning local authority is not easily built. There are many obstacles to learning. So the first step is to learn about how the authority learns and how it does not learn. And then ...:

- The local authority is guarded by powerful organisational walls. While boundaries have to be protected, they can be over-protected. More openings are required.
- Hierarchies remove learning. They have to be by-passed, at least occasionally.
- Channels of communication carry their own distortion. Distortion cannot be avoided, but it can be guarded against.
- Many channels carry many distortions, but that is better than the single distortion.
- In traditional management learning supports the existing patterns of service. A new learning is required, that can allow the possibility of new patterns of service.
- Against dominant organisational tendencies, countervailing channels of communication and of knowledge must be built.
- There is more knowledge than can be carried by professional channels.
- There are more ways of mapping the environment than by the existing pattern of service delivery.
- Trends build counter-trends; ideas cannot be held within past trends.
- The organisation must pause to reflect on its learning.

# 6

# Challenge and Choice in Policy Analysis

## THE NEED FOR CHALLENGE

The new management has to challenge existing policy and the practices that derive from that policy. It challenges in order to expose choice, where traditional management sees no scope for choice, because thinking is constrained by assumptions formed by present practice. Those assumptions support the provision of existing services but limit local government by concealing choice.

There are powerful organisational interests structured around present practice, both within the authority and without. Such interests defend present practice, if challenged. Yet challenge is rare. There is a perceived necessity about present practice in local authorities. An existing activity undertaken by the authority gives expression to a set of assumptions about the need for the activity, the appropriate way of providing the activity and the way that provision should be organised. These assumptions will rarely be made explicit, because they do not need to be in the day-to-day requirements of traditional management.

The procedures of the local authority and its structure give expression to these organisational assumptions. The structures identify and group activities. The procedures reinforce the assumption of need, since inevitably external demand tends to be categorised as the need the authority is structured to meet. The staff are trained to meet that need in a particular way, and for professionals that training provides their identity and their status.

Structure, procedures and training give an apparent necessity to present practice. It is difficult to think outside that practice, when it is reinforced by the very working of the authority. The professional culture allows no place for challenge to the practice that has formed the culture. A committee agenda is formed by present practice.

Limits are, in effect, placed on organisational thinking.

The privatisation debate, which has really been a debate about private contracting, challenges organisational assumptions. It challenges the assumption that because a function has been given to local government the service involved has to be provided directly by the local authority. Thus until recently it was as if the very words 'refuse collection' meant direct provision of the service. That represented the limit of organisational experience. Any alternative lay outside the boundaries of organisational thinking. There was no reason why a perspective formed by traditional management should challenge that assumption.

Those assumptions have, however, been challenged by the political process. The organisational assumption that direct provision of service is the mode through which services are discharged is being replaced by the assumption that the only alternative is private contracting. That alternative has been rejected by many local authorities, but may well be enforced by government legislation.

Other local authorities could provide services. Legal support for Chester-Le-Street District Council is provided by the County Council at 'a negotiated price two thirds of the standard fee for normal work' (Mobbs, 1982, p. 123). Community groups, voluntary organisations or organised volunteers could provide services. A service could be provided by a workers co-operative or a professional partnership. In Sunderland, Little Women is a thirteen strong cleaning co-operative providing a home-help service, drawing finance from DHSS money for supplementary benefits claimants towards the cost of domestic help, but with the support of the social services department (*Guardian*, 6.8.85).

The direct provision of services is an organisational assumption that underlies the general activities of the local authority. There are equally powerful assumptions underlying particular activities. Present practice is not merely thought of as the best practice, but *the* practice.

Local authorities have many inspectorate functions: building, fire prevention, trading standards, environmental health, etc. The way these inspectorate functions are allocated in the organisation is in part a product of the division of local authorities' functions between two tiers of government with, for example, trading standards in the Shire areas being a county function, while environmental health is a district function. That is not the only basis of division. An organisational division between, for example, trading standards and environmental health existed in many London Boroughs. Recently a number of these boroughs have created combined departments. The Chief Environmental and Consumer Services Officer of Islington has concluded there are major gains in joint action, exchange of information and in relations with consumers (Banfield, 1985, p. 24).

Yet other more radical changes in organisation are possible. It would be possible to have a general-purpose environmental inspectorate, embracing some or all of the inspectorate functions, backed by specialist services where required. Such proposals lie beyond dominant organisational assumptions and are, therefore, beyond organisational thinking. They do not normally enter the realm of consideration. Westminster City Council which is reviewing their inspectorate services is marked out as one exception.

There is a terrible necessity in organisation practice. The assumptions by which experience is organised are not easily challenged – a library had to be silent; a swimming pool had to be rectangular; a bus had to have a conductor. Past practice built assumptions that proved hard to challenge.

> The public library's tradition of 'passive' service is also likely to affect its success in providing service to local government ... The main purpose of public libraries was considered to be the collection, organisation and storage of documents for the benefit of those members of the community who were willing and able to come to the library. It was not the exploitation of documents for those who wanted information and even today public libraries tend to be very much self-help services.
>
> (Grayson, 1978, pp. 48–49)

Past traditions are not easily overcome.


## THE FOCUS FOR ATTENTION

For organisational assumptions to be the subject of challenge, they have first to be the focus of attention. Traditional management does not normally focus attention on the assumptions which underlie its practice, for it has no need to do so. Indeed to do so would interfere with the task of service provision.

It would be wrong to assume that challenge does not now take place. It has three main sources. There is, as we have seen in the privatisation debate, a political challenge. Yet that political challenge has too often been weakened because of the dominance of the requirements of service provision. The attention of key political actors, as service chairs, become focused on those requirements. Political challenge, even when present, can become weakened by the lack of organisational leverage to turn political purpose into effective organisational action.

Challenge can come from the officer structure. Within that structure individual officers have ideas that challenge explicitly or implicitly organisational assumptions. The problem is to find the organisational time and space to develop them and the organisational protection to establish them. A chief officer can provide a basis for innovation that challenges organisational assumptions, provided he or she can separate themselves from the routines of service provision. Yet chief officers, as are any officers, are limited by roles, which have certain assumptions built into them. It is hard to think and act outside one's role.'

External events can bring so forceful a challenge that they can secure attention. The problem too often is that the local authority is protected against the external environment so that it is only when external events create major pressures that they can secure attention. A screaming point has to be reached. At that point, the organisational barriers can no longer exclude reality. A tragedy in child care, a Ronan Point explosion, can focus attention and can enforce organisational change. Growing public protest can reach a point where it must be heard. Financial pressures growing in scale can require scrutiny of much that was previously taken for granted. Attention is not always contained within organisational assumptions. Challenge, although hard to establish, is possible, even within traditional management.

For the new management, challenge should be greater. Political challenge should not so easily be overwhelmed or suffocated in the routines. Officer challenge should be more readily heard.

The processes of learning can focus attention on issues. Learning processes can identify issues, unheard through existing communiction channels. It is not enough, however, to focus attention on issues. The organisation must be capable of thought about the issues from a governmental perspective rather than an operational perspective. It must not be limited by the apparent necessity of present practice. Organisational assumptions have to be challenged if choice is to be exposed.

## POLICY ANALYSIS AS NEW THINKING

In this chapter policy analysis will be set out as a way of thinking about an authority's policy and practice that can challenge organisational assumptions, expose choices and assist judgement on those choices. Policy analysis is, at its simplest, a way of thinking about policy and practice that differs from those dominant in its organisation. It can, therefore, take many different forms dependent on what is dominant in an organisation. Policy analysis is countervailing thought that challenges the organisational taken-for-granted 'carefully evaluating all bits of "conventional" wisdom that derive their authority from repetition, familiarity or associated with high officialdom' (Downs, 1976, p. 3).

There is no one form of policy analysis. Its form varies from organisation to organisation, depending on the ways of thinking that are dominant in the organisation. The requirement is that it adds new ways of thinking. Since local authorities normally consider issues on functional terms, policy analysis should consider issues on other terms: for example, in terms of area or clients. If local authorities were organised on an area basis, then policy analysis would consider issues on functional terms. In this book policy analysis adds to local authorities conditioned by the necessities of service provision, the challenge and the choice that derives from their role as local government.

The rational model of decision-making has been regarded as providing a model for policy analysis. The rational model can, of course, never be applied in all its purity. It is usually, therefore, set out in a modified form. The local authority:

(1) identifies needs and problems, present and foreseen, in its environment;
(2) sets its objectives in relation to those needs;
(3) considers alternative ways of meeting those objectives;
(4) evaluates those alternatives in terms of their use of resources and of their effects;
(5) makes decisions in the light of that evaluation;
(6) translates those decisions into management action.

The rational model is not a model for policy analysis. That is to misunderstand its role. The rational model, as I have argued elsewhere (Stewart, 1982), is not helpful in suggesting how to carry out policy analysis. It does not suggest how policy alternatives are derived, how those alternatives are crafted into implementable alternatives, or how they are judged in situations of conflicting objectives. The rational model does not explain how to carry out policy analysis. Its role is different. The rational model provides a framework to test and to justify policy. Its influence is more on how policy is presented than on how policy is worked on.

For local government, local authorities need new ways of thinking that can lead to choice in policy and practice. The new ways of thinking must, if they are to lead to new choice for the local authority, differ from those established in the organisation and yet be capable of leading to realistic policy options. Judgement on these policy options is required and that depends upon the political process.

Emphasis will be placed on those ways of thinking that challenge existing ways of thinking:

- on understanding the policy area, beyond the necessities of service provision;
- deriving policy options beyond present organisational assumptions;
- supporting political judgement on local choice.

## UNDERSTANDING THE POLICY AREA

To derive new policy or to change existing policy requires understanding, not merely of that policy, but of the environment on and in which it operates. Both the external environment and the organisational environment have to be understood.

Understanding the policy area is an essential step towards policy design and the preparation of policy options. Each policy area has its own characteristics that are not adequately described in the identification of needs and problems. The shape of the policy area has to be discerned.

The process can be illustrated by a series of questions about the policy area:

*(1) Constraints*
What are the perceived constraints on action by the authority? How far are those constraints real? Could they be modified given time and effort?

What are the present resources (finance, but also manpower, building land and equipment), and what are the constraints on change or on development of those resources?

What are the limitations on knowledge about the policy areas? What approaches are ruled out by political or public values?

*(2) Interests*
What interests are concerned in the policy area, and how far is there agreement or disagreement between those interests:

- inside the local authority?
- in the community?

Can present lines of conflict or consensus be modified? Who gains or who loses from existing policy or lack of policy?

### (3) Assumptions

What are the assumptions that underlie existing policy or lack of policy:

- about the way people behave?
- about the effects of existing policy?
- about the relationships between action taken and impact?

Are these assumptions valid?

What systems of belief support those assumptions and are those beliefs widely shared? What interests support those beliefs?

### (4) Environmental Change

Are the issues at stake in the policy area changing, and in what direction? Will change provoke counter-change?

How will those changes affect existing interests?

What are the perceived certainties and uncertainties in the direction of change?

### (5) Behaviour Patterns

What are the dominant patterns of social, economic or physical patterns of behaviour that affect or are affected by the policy areas?

How far can these patterns of behaviour be modified by the actions of the authority?

There are no final answers to many of these questions. They are designed to encourage a way of thinking rather than to secure closure. Behind such questions lies a recognition that a policy area is not a blank sheet on which policy analysis can write at will. There is either present policy, or lack of stated policy, which may itself be a policy.

Positions will be at stake which are defended by existing organisational interests. There is much at stake in present practice. Thus not merely have proposals for contracting out been strongly opposed by staff, but also proposals for decentralisation to area offices. Some anticipate that they must lose by any change. Others hope to gain.

There are limits to the possibilities of change. There are actual constraints, but there are also perceived constraints. The 'myth of statutory constraint' (Stewart, 1983, p. 146) has protected services against cuts in expenditure. It has been argued, by those concerned to protect services, that most existing expenditure is mandatory on an authority. In practice analysis shows the room for choice is much wider than normally allowed.

While assumptions about the nature of statutory constraints has protected existing services, they have also limited local authority initiatives. Statutory powers have been interpreted by present practice rather than by future possibility. Yet the problems highlighted by the new politics have challenged past assumptions and opened up new possibilities for action and influence. Thus in a recent pamphlet published by the Low Pay Unit, it has been argued that:

> Local authorities need not remain passive observers of the low pay problem. Although councils cannot be held responsible for the problem, there is much that they can do to alleviate its effect on local residents and the local economy.
>
> (Pond, p. 30)

The pamphlet considers the contribution that can be made to overcome the problem of low pay by economic, industrial and employment policies, attempts to improve the employment conditions and status of disadvantaged groups, recommended pay guidelines, local authorities as employers, contracts with private firms and local campaigns.

Policy analysis is grounded in politics. That does not mean that the analysis should be restricted in its scope or should obscure unpalatable facts. Rather it means that it must recognise that a policy area is value ridden, that decisions do not spring merely from objectively stated facts, as any councillor or officer faced with the problems of the location of a children's home or a school closure knows well.

There are different values at stake and different interests supportive of such values. The building up of the understanding of the policy area, marked by conflict as well as consensus, challenges the unitary model of society which traditional management has assumed. The plotting of the policy area proposed here is a first step in policy analysis. It does not rule out the more commonly accepted work of policy analysis in identifying the problem and seeking data about it. Such analysis is of little value in a political institution, however, unless set against the plotting of the policy area described above.

## POLICY DERIVATION AND DESIGN

The most difficult task in policy analysis and the least commented on is the derivation and design of new policies, whether in response to a new problem or as an alternative to existing policies.

Policy analysis as a discipline has generally focused on methods for the assessment of policy alternatives, with some concessions in the direction of policy definition, criteria specification and feasibility analysis. The imagery is normally that of considered choice between a number of alternatives based on a well-defined set of goals. In its standard formulations this model says nothing about the generation or crafting of alternatives, only their scrutiny. This omission is paradoxical, inasmuch as the primary role of the policy analyst in government, is, empirically, that of 'ideas person', responsible for coming up with offers.

(Dryzek, 1983)

The role of policy analysis is to break through the constraints of organisational thought. Existing practice imprisons organisational thought. Organisational assumptions and perceived constraints define the limits of the practical. Plotting the policy area exposes assumptions and challenges perceived constraints. Yet the hard work of deriving and designing policies has still to be carried out.

Within established organisational assumptions and constraints there may be little scope for new policies. The problem is to break out of the necessity of the present. Organisational assumptions and constraints that act as boundaries limiting thought have to be leapt over, as when the Devon library service redefined its role as extending beyond traditional library services to the provision of 'an integrated communication network' and 'publishing' (Shute, 1983, pp. 33–38).

It would be wrong to expect a set of rules for the derivation of policy. Rather than rules, alternative modes of thinking about policy are suggested.

## Suspension of Disbelief

Techniques can help to break through the necessity of the present and encourage the challenging of existing assumptions and perceived constraints. Most of these techniques depend upon the suspension of disbelief for a sufficient period of time to permit new ideas to emerge and grow. Protection is required from the harsh voice of practicality. The impractical idea needs encouragement to become the practical proposal.

New alternatives and new possibilities do not arise through systematic and elaborate analysis. New ideas emerge more often from the unexpected combination of events or data. Brain-storming is the prototype of techniques to stimulate ideas. It requires that the group list ideas for resolving a problem, and as many ideas as possible – sensible and idiotic, routine or bizarre – are put forward in a short period of time. Wild idea stimulates wild idea. The one procedural rule is that in brain-storming, there is no judgement, no critical comment and no evaluation. The role of the chair is to enforce that rule, and only that rule. Ideas must have sufficient leeway to establish themselves and to stimulate. Then, and only then, can ideas be sifted and pursued. The limits of perceived practicality are driven back.

The suspension of disbelief can be encouraged in other ways. Scenarios of the future permit the relaxing of present constraints. What appears impossible now in the awareness of practical immediacies may seem less improbable if considered for the future. New technology can stimulate thought, provided it is not constrained by assumptions based on present practice. Thus as cable television makes an impact, it has been argued that not only will

> local authorities be able to benefit from its possibilities but community life may change in ways that are not necessarily predictable.
>
> (Wedgwood-Oppenheim and Baddeley, 1983, p. 62)

Once the possibility for the future is admitted, consideration can be given to the pathways that could lead from the present to the future. It may only be possible to discern those pathways from the present, if one has already gained a sense of direction from possibilities in the future.

*Different and Differing Perspectives*
The derivation and design of new policies require challenge to the dominant perspective, from those with different and differing perspectives. Thought about policy-making can be extended by bringing new perspectives to policy consideration in inter-disciplinary working groups. Ways of thinking about transportation issues can be challenged and extended by a working group that consists not merely of planners, engineers and public transport managers, but contains social workers, education officers and environmental health officers, because they can bring different ways of thinking to those accustomed to past ways of working.

For the new management a main source of challenge comes from the political process. Politics brings a perspective that can differ sharply from the perspective of service provision. From that perspective emerge ideas which need development by policy analysis. Organisational space is needed for that development.

The political manifesto can be a rich source for the derivation of policy ideas, not least when the ideas are 'totally unrealistic', which may merely mean that the ideas challenge existing organisational assumptions. Ideas for user control can easily be dismissed as involving unnecessary risks; decentralising financial responsibility to schools has been attacked as weakening proper financial control. 'Unrealistic ideas' should be worked on; their alleged unrealism teased out; new alternatives built around them. Political values can be used as a starting point for new policies. A belief in the market, a belief in redistributive policies, a value on public involvement, a policy for equal opportunities, each can suggest alternative approaches to present practices. Councillors can play an active role in the generation of policy options. Working groups set up as part of policy analysis to explore such options need ready access to the political viewpoint which can best be secured by councillor membership of such groups. In Strathclyde social services committee such groups played an important role in policy innovation and there are now examples from many authorities.

The field-workers who confront the environment directly can bring to policy analysis a perspective which differs from that of management at the centre of the local authority, but which is often unexpressed in existing channels of communication. Policy analysis needs to draw on that perspective as well as on the perspective of those at the centre of the authority. The more initiative and experiment can be encouraged by field-workers the more there is for policy analysis to learn from differing practices and experiences.

Local authorities can and do learn from the ideas and the practice of other authorities, although the learning normally follows well defined professional channels. They can learn from their trade unions, who contribute ideas which can otherwise be neglected. There are other organisations – private sector and voluntary – which could suggest new approaches to policy and practice.

Perhaps the least used source of ideas are the public of the authority. Local authorities are themselves dominated by 'producer advocates' (Downs, 1976); consumer advocacy is too weakly articulated, even by councillors transformed into producer advocates by their role on service committees.

A local authority that emphasises public service and learning seeks from the public complaints, ideas and suggestions about its services. The public can be directly involved in policy issues. The Nottingham Community Project, working with county and district authorities, organised consumer involvement in a county review of the provision for childrens plays (Neilson, 1984, pp. 89–91).

More, much more, is required than one-off consultation. That may well frustrate more than help. As a report for Halton District Council says:

Genuine and full consultation requires public involvement in decisions that affect their immediate neighbourhood. It requires that everyone at least has the opportunity to put forward their points of view. It requires that if circumstances change after a decision is made, or if delays occur, then this information is fed back to those concerned. In other words, consultation is a continuous and not a one-off event. If residents do not feel involved in a decision or they feel it has been forced on them, then this can increase any feeling of alienation that may already exist between the public and authority in general.

(Stevens, 1983, p. 38)

Policy alternatives can be extended by increasing the sources from which ideas are sought to those which are not conditioned by the limitations imposed by traditional management. Many of the ideas will be dismissed as impractical, but if disbelief is suspended, they could be a source from which practical alternatives can be developed.

### A Challenge to Assumptions
Policy analysis has to challenge the assumptive world of service provision. Within that assumptive world traditional management justifies itself in present practice.

By focusing on the taken for granted, the policy analyst can challenge the apparent necessity of present practice. Reconsideration of the taken for granted is difficult for those within the assumptive world of operational management. The taken for granted is taken for granted. Perspectives from outside the organisational assumptions can bring awareness for those within.

A new viewpoint generates new alternatives. Approaches developed in the United States to rethinking service delivery illustrate that challenge. Large scale action has often been seen as an organisational necessity and organisational thinking restricted to a centralist approach.

If you decide to use an alternative approach, you need to think it through carefully. This may seem like a minor point. You need to understand well and be committed to an alternative approach. As you find yourself being drawn in, be prepared to do the most difficult thing an individual (or organization) can be asked to do: change his basic way of thinking.

First, you'll need a noncentralist view of the way communities work. Actually, it isn't the service professional, public or private, who ultimately keeps streets clean and safe; it is the way people decide to behave. For example, a city cannot keep streets clean if people walk along shedding paper. Similarly, doctors cannot keep patients healthy if they are not concerned about nutrition and exercise; teachers cannot educate kids who do not want to learn.

If there are dog bites in the neighbourhood, residents may not think it necessary immediately to obtain more or better doctors. They may suggest paying neighbourhood kids $5 apiece to round up the stray dogs. Residents may then come to you for the money you don't need to spend on doctors. Why shouldn't they get it? Most people first think about informal non-professional, law-capital approaches to problems. Governments should, but frequently don't.

*Small beginnings are best.*

The question of scale can also be an important issue. Most alternative service delivery approaches have small beginnings. Many people in government are unaccustomed to solving problems through small scale action. Understandably, they know that it is more expensive for them to rehabilitate one house at a time than a project at a time, or to administer 100 contracts for refuse collection rather than just one comprehensive contract. How will the big job ever get done? If it's a big job, isn't a big organization needed? So when considering alternative service delivery options, one needs a special attitude to conceive a big job getting done through a large aggregation of individual, small actions. This is precisely the way much of the progress is being made in energy conservation. America is getting insulated one house at a time.

Kolderie, 1983, pp. 44–45; reprinted from *Public Management Magazine*, October 1982 by special permission, © 1982, The International City Management Association, Washington, D.C.)

If a new viewpoint is found, and new assumptions are made, then new alternatives will be found.


## NEW INSTRUMENTS OF POLICY

Traditional management uses well established instruments of policy. The staff are trained to use those instruments. A social worker carries out case work in a professionally accepted way. An environmental health officer carries out inspection according to accepted professional practice. The skills available become the policy instruments available, limiting thought about alternative policy. Where the local authority confronts new issues it uses the policy instruments available or moulds new policy instruments on past instruments. Thus when structure plans and local plans were introduced to explore the former development plans the degree of innovation was less than hoped for. The new plans were drawn up by planners conditioned to the policy instruments they knew.

To consider policy instruments which are but little used by local authorities can be a way of deriving new thinking about policy. The policy suggests the instrument, but the instrument can also suggest the policy. Local authorities have available the instrument of influence. Established as the local government for an area, based on elected authority, with a multitude of contact points and a wide range of powers and duties, the authority can influence even where it cannot act. A local authority can influence health authorities even though it cannot provide a health service. Effective influence has to be managed, as has action. Influence is a resource that can be built up or dissipated. Influence can also be neglected. To consider influence as a policy instrument extends thought on policy alternatives. Birmingham's attempt to secure the Olympic Games is an exercise in the management of influence on a world-wide scale. A local authority's opposition to the closure of local post offices as part of its policy for rural communities is an exercise in the management of influence on a local scale.

Marketing is another neglected policy instrument, although used imaginatively by some authorities, such as, for example, Bradford in its promotion of the city as a tourist centre (Fenn, 1983). In their 1984 Annual Report, the Audit Commission comments on the relative under-development of marketing in fields as diverse as courses in further education, school meals and leisure centres (Audit Commission Commission, 1984a). The reasons appear obvious. A local authority is often more constrained to ration demand than to increase its market. That does not, however, rule out the use of market research to ensure services meet user requirements, or of marketing techniques to ensure the services are obtained by those most in need. 'Demarketing' may have a role in adjusting demand to resources available.

> While most marketing experts are in the business of encouraging and building up demand for an organization's products or services, a major task of public managers in these times of scarcity is often to stretch their meagre resources, trying to make sure that there is enough left of the shrinking pie to give all their clients some amount, however reduced. They are not trying to attract customers for their programs. In some other cases (e.g. energy or water conservation ...) the aim is to dampen public demand or limit usage to only 'essential' customers and activities as a matter of public policy. Demarketing – the use of marketing strategies to

reduce demand or channel it to appropriate uses – can be helpful here.

(Goodrich, 1983, p. 101)

Demarketing opens up possibilities, by freeing thought about marketing from its conventional limits.

If marketing is seen as understanding and influencing public behaviour, then marketing approaches can contribute to problems such as those below, only some of which would normally be thought of as marketing problems:

- use of public transport
- take up of rate rebates (or welfare benefits generally);
- litter in city centres;
- pricing and products in the school meals service;
- prompt payment of rates;
- truancy;
- electoral turnout;
- access to council facilities by the deprived.

New instruments stimulate new thinking about policy alternatives. Without new instruments thought comes back to existing instruments, and existing policy.

*The Telling of Policy Stories*

A good policy has a good story. Indeed the telling of a good story may be an important step in the derivation of policy alternatives:

> The giving of advice and the design of social programmes is like the telling of relevant stories. Such stories resemble proverbs and metaphors, for they seek to match reality to archetypal patterns of events by drawing analogies. That is to say, they provide an interpretation of a complex pattern of events with normative implications for action ...

(Rein, 1976, p. 266)

A new policy needs a new story that is sufficiently convincing to replace old stories and change the assumptive world. A policy story is grounded in policy understanding and grows out of the mapping of the policy area. A policy story must have meaning in the political process, helping the politician to see and to explain.

New stories have their impact if they 'explain' policy stress – the failure of existing policy to cope with emerging problems. The Buchanan Report in 1963 on 'Traffic in Towns', provided a new story for transportation policy. Environmentalists have provided a volume of stories which carry increasing conviction. Their stories 'explain' the destruction of living lakes and forests. Their stories are changing assumptive worlds, showing new policy choices and suggesting how they might be designed.

Policy analysts must be good story tellers if they are to help change assumptive worlds. They can learn much from the slogan writers who know how from complexity to produce simplicity in significance. The best slogans express good stories. The environmentalists have learnt their slogan from their stories. 'Save our forests' is a policy for new forms of refuse collection and of pollution control. 'Clean air' went far both to suggest and to secure smoke control policies.

## SUPPORTING POLITICAL JUDGEMENT

In the final resort judgements have to be made and in a local authority those judgements reflect political choice. Judgement cannot be avoided by processes of analysis based on the prediction of the likely effect of policy alternatives and the assessment of that effect against stated objectives. Political choice cannot be reduced to a calculation.

Prediction can be difficult and becomes more difficult the more radical the policy alternatives. Predictions are made on the basis of past experience. As a proposal differs from past experience, prediction can become less reliable. Judgement has to replace prediction and judgement must face the balance between the risks of the unpredictable against the over-caution of the predictable.

Asessment against assumed or stated objectives may merely reveal the need for judgement. Policy alternatives may aid the achievement of one objective, but not another. Even that may over-simplify. Policy choices involves gainers and losers. There are costs and benefits. Some values will be forwarded by a policy alternative, others may be weakened. Some interests may support the policy alternative; others may oppose it. Evaluation cannot reduce choice to calculation. Judgement is involved in the choice on the balance of conflicting values and interest.

Judgement is a weighing of different factors: risk and caution; relative certainty and relative uncertainty; supporting and opposing interests; inflexibility and flexibility; values to be attained and values to be denied. Judgement can be informed by policy analysis, but it cannot be predetermined.

Judgement in local government is political judgement. It will and should be guided by political values. Any process of policy analysis to guide judgement should take account of those values. Policy analysis should draw upon understanding of the policy area. The plotting of interests and of constraints, of assumptions made and assumptions challenged, are critical to judgement.

Judgement is aided if analysis provides even tentative answers to such questions as:

* How reliable are the assumptions on which the policy proposal is based?
* Do those assumptions differ from previously accepted assumptions?
* How robust is the policy in the event of change in the assumptions?
* How many staff inside the organisation have their role changed by the proposal?
* How difficult will they find that change?
* On how many implementation points does the policy depend?
* How difficult will the policy be to implement?
* What is the anticipated change, if any, in social behaviour required by the policy?
* Does the proposal follow, modify or challenge existing policy?
* Who gains and who loses from the proposed policy?
* Which organisational and environmental interests oppose and which support the proposal?
* How near is the proposed policy to present policy?
* What constraints have to be overcome?

The answers to these questions do not constitute judgement; they assist judgement.

Judgement is not for policy analysis but for politics; policy analysis can assist or strengthen judgement.

Judgement can be aided if certain guidelines are respected. They do not constitute good judgement, but they can assist it.

## *Do Not Expect More of Analysis than It Can Provide*

Analysis cannot provide experience of what has not been experienced. Analysis informs but does not resolve the dilemma of political choice. The dilemma is in part a choice between conflicting values, but it is heightened by uncertainty and that involves risk which can impose political costs.

The risks are often greater than they need be because of uniformity. A policy change in the past has often been a change adopted throughout the area of the authority and for that reason, once made, not easily abandoned.

Judgement of the novel could be assisted if experience could be gained by experiments. Early experiments in pedestrianisation of shopping streets disarmed many shopkeepers' fears of loss of custom. There, experiment seemed natural. In the building of the high-rise flats, commitment outran experience.

Because the principle of uniformity governs service provision, experiments are resisted. Where a degree of diversity replaces uniformity, varying experience provides its own experiment and judgement can grow through trial and error.

### Simplicity Is a Merit
A simple policy is a policy more likely to be understood. Refinements are better made by responsiveness in practice rather than over-elaboration in anticipation. A simple policy is a policy more likely to be correctly judged politically. Conformity to political values may be lost in complexity. Thus the rate support grant system has increasingly escaped from political judgement to complexity.

### A Good Story Makes a Good Policy
That may be going too far. At least one can say a bad story is unlikely to mean a good policy. A story shows how policy links to understanding of the policy area. It links events to activities proposed. If that cannot be done, then the policy should be judged out of court. It will never even be understood by those who have to carry it out.

### Judge Not by the Unitary Model Alone
The political process requires judgement not merely against a unitary model of society alone, but against the model of a society of differing and different interests. One can ask, as Brent Council requires, all policy proposals before committees to indicate the race relations and gender implications.

### Testing Out Values
Values are made explicit in judgement upon proposals. Testing out values in proposals can mean modifying and adjusting proposals to separate the acceptable from the unacceptable. 'The road line was not rejected because of the agricultural land taken alone; that merely tipped the balance against a proposal that still did not fully solve the congestion problems in the town.' To interpret the key value as agricultural land is to be misled.

### One Can Always Ask the People
It could help! Local authorities struggling with choices between rate rises and expenditure cuts might be surprised by the results. Surveys

carried out in authorities have shown a readiness to accept rate rises, rather than cuts in services (Game, 1983, pp. 26–32).

*A Robust Policy Has Strength in a Changing World*
A proposal that will meet not merely present circumstances, but a range of circumstances, has special merit in changing times. A building that can be easily adapted to new purposes can the more easily meet changing circumstances. Judgement can be assisted by testing proposals against various assumptions of relevant change.

# CONCLUSION

Policy analysis adds new thinking and, in that new thinking, challenges. That is its contribution. Policy analysis can be carried out by all those who can bring new thinking. It can be carried out by councillors, by chief officers, by middle management, by field-workers, or by members of the public. Policy analysis considers policy from a differing perspective to that dominant in the organisation. The issue may be less who carries it out, but the source of support for the analysis, for analysis challenges established organisational interests.

Policy analysis can gain strength only from countervailing interests to those dominant in existing activities. Those interests will often be based on the political process. On such a basis can challenge be mounted to established organisational interests.

Policy analysis has been presented an an alternative mode of thought to the ways of thinking conditioned by traditional management. Its value almost lies in that difference rather than in the particular mode of thought. Emphasis has been placed on:

- understanding the shape of the policy area;
- breaking the boundaries of thought in policy design;
- the art of judgement being given primacy over evaluation.

What has been written is about a style of thinking that escapes routinisation.

- To understand the interests that lie in wait is necessary for the unwary traveller in policy space.
- One must seek out the too easily taken for granted.
- Many perceived constraints are not actual constraints.
- For the delicate plant of new ideas to grow protection is required.
- Organisational thought runs along the channels laid by the routines of practice; new thinking demands new channels.

- In a different assumptive world, the impossible becomes possible and the unthinkable can be thought about.
- New policies can be found in new stories.
- Evaluation carried to the point of precision does not aid judgement but prevents it.
- To judge is to weigh not one factor but many.
- There is a need for judgement to use experiment and the learning from difference.
- In the complex of differing interests there can be many judgements, but choice depends on the political process.

# 7

# Direction and Choice in Policy Processes

## THE REQUIREMENTS FOR A POLICY PERSPECTIVE

Traditional management focuses on service provision. It is concerned with the operations necessary for service provision and with improvement of the methods used, where possible and appropriate. The dominant perspective is an operational perspective, in which concern with policy is a distraction from the task in hand. It would be a distraction and a confusion to suggest that there was a choice as to whether the operations should be carried out at all or as to the purposes they were intended to achieve. Those who have work to do, will not consider themselves helped if they have to spend much time considering whether the work is necessary.

The new management requires a perspective that differs from the operational perspective of traditional management. That perspective must focus on the learning and the challenge described in the last chapters, to enable them to be established in the working of the local authority. That perspective must also focus on the role of the local authority as local government, giving direction to its activities in relations to the problems of the area it governs.

The required perspective can be described as a policy perspective, since it looks beyond the activities undertaken to the policies that could be pursued.

A policy perspective does not replace an operational perspective. Both are required. The policy perspective complements the operational perspective. A local authority that does not have an operational perspective does not deliver. A local authority that does not have a policy perspective does not govern.

A policy perspective needs organisational protection against the dominance of the operational perspective because of its immediacy and because of the necessary concentration of much managerial time and energy on its requirements. Operational management has a timetable of urgency. Policy can wait. That is why protection is needed.

The required policy perspective derives from the nature of local government in a changing environment. The policy perspective will sustain:

- *the primacy of the political process* over the operational requirements of service provision;
- *the recognition of choice* rather than the continuities of existing activities;
- a concern not merely for the short term of immediate action, but for the *longer-term horizon of choice*;
- a perspective that looks beyond the services provided *towards the environment* of problems and opportunities;
- a recognition that local authorities are at the heart of *a network of government*, rather than the isolated providers of a series of separate services.
- *an awareness of uncertainty* rather than the certainty of continuing activities;
- *a selectivity of policy* rather than the comprehensiveness of operational activity;
- *a sense of direction* rather than the routinisation of present activities;
- *a protected pause* in on-going processes of traditional management.

Policy processes in local authorities can give support to a policy perspective. The considerations that should guide those processes are explored in this chapter.

## THE PRIMACY OF POLITICAL PROCESS

The new management of local government recognises the primacy of the political process in local government. Policy processes have to protect the primacy of politics against the depoliticising operational perspective.

The political process has its own timetable and its own time-scale, based on the electoral cycle. A local authority's four year electoral cycle with an all-in/all-out election can be reflected by the policy processes. An all-out election marks a significant point in time, likely to involve change in council membership even if not necessarily in party control. A newly elected council needs to take stock, and to set directions for its period of office.

In metropolitan districts and in certain shire districts, where a third of the council retire each year (except in the fourth year when county elections are, or in metropolitan areas were, held), the significance of the electoral cycle can vary. Only at certain elections will there be a likelihood of control changing. In these authorities the policy planning processes must be sufficiently flexible to link to the realistic electoral cycle. Party manifestos can indicate when a significant change of direction takes place.

Manifestos are becoming important documents in the political process, prepared in detail by local political parties to set directions for an authority. For the new management of local government, the manifesto must be a key document, the base from which policy processes develop.

Where there is no manifesto beyond the generalities of the general rhetoric of national politics untranslatable into local action, there is a danger of no political direction. Policy statements, prepared politically, can help to provide an alternative starting point for the policy process in such authorities.

In a hung authority the manifestos remain important for the policy processes. From the manifestos areas of agreement and disagreement can be plotted. Policies which have a majority support in the council can be identified.

The crucial problem for the policy processes lies in the relationship between manifestos (or their equivalent) and the actual circumstances — financial and otherwise — in which an authority finds itself. It may not be possible to implement the whole of a manifesto in the lifetime of the council; not all the manifesto will be clear enough for implementation, nor is it necessarily immutable in changing circumstances. Traditional management has often encouraged cynicism about manifesto and a budget — and the two contradict each other. The new management must confront that contradiction, not in cynicism but to establish where change is required. Key areas of difficulty can be identified. Choice can be highlighted as to how far, or in what ways, the manifesto should be met, and as to the priorities and the timing of change.

The important point is to start the policy process, with a political input either from the manifesto or from a policy statement, uncontaminated by the apparent imperatives of traditional management. If the policy process starts from perceived constraints, it will never get beyond them. Yet policies, although grounded in politics, have still to be capable of being translated into activities to be undertaken. The policy processes have to relate the language of politics to the language of the officer structure. The political process provides the starting point, but more is required.

The officer input into the policy processes comes in recon-
ciliation between policy and action, or between politics and operational 'necessities', which may well prove to be no better and no
worse than the unfounded assumptions of past practice. The
officer input must be in a form which is meaningful politically,
and which can be used by councillors in the settings in which
policy will be made. This involves officers understanding their
own assumptions and values, particularly where they run counter
to political priorities. This is not easily achieved. It is not easy for
land-use planners to recognise their own values in differentiated
densities of development recommended, or for social services
officers to recognise when they substitute their own values for
those of the client. It is hard for a treasurer to recognise the
political content of inflation assumptions or for education officers
to accept the political nature of their judgement on secondary
reorganisation. Value sensitivity and political awareness should
mark the contribution of the officer to the policy process. This
does not necessarily imply political commitment by the officer.
Political neutrality is more likely to be preserved by those who are
politically aware, rather than by those who blunder unknowingly
into political positions.

Policy is not determined by objective factors alone. It involves
values held and values rejected. Policy processes are based on the
primacy of politics will involve conflict and controversy. That is not
to be regretted, but welcomed. Conflict and controversy command
attention. Many a local authority has in the past produced statements of objectives with which nobody could disagree and hence
had little impact.

> To provide an opportunity for all residents of the Borough to live
> in satisfactory homes in pleasant surroundings at a price that
> families can afford.
>
> (Islington, 1971)

Set apart from time and resources they raised no issues for political
choice. Not merely did they have no political content, they had little
content at all, being acceptable in their generality to everyone. They
gave no direction to the authority. Direction implies not merely
going in one direction, but rejecting others. It involves choosing to
support certain values, rather than others. It involves political
choice, and political choice involves controversy.

# THE RECOGNITION OF CHOICE

The present pattern of activities in a local authority represents past choice, frozen into present practice. Policy processes for the new management expose choice in the present and in the future, even if the choice taken is to re-affirm the present. It shows that what is need not be, and what might be could be. The new management does not take as sacrosanct present levels or methods of service.

In so far as there are constraints on choice, the policy processes should expose them. If statutory requirements mean that a particular service has to be provided, if present building, staffing skills or trade union attitudes, impose constraints, then that has to be exposed in an analysis of constraints.

The issues raised by such an analysis of constraints are whether perceived constraints are real and permanent, or whether they could, given time and effort, be overcome. Staff can be retrained, new buildings can be built, trade union attitudes modified, given time. Even legislation can be repealed or amended. If they are real, or if the constraint is accepted (i.e. chosen), then within those constraints lies the space for choice.

Choice between services and on the form of the services involves value choice. It may be argued that choice and value choice are alien to the political process – and that far from seeking to expose choice and make explicit the values underlying the choice, councillors prefer management processes that limit choice. If the present provision of services is statutorily required, then councillors can hardly be criticised for their cost. The assumption is that there are less political costs in evading responsibilities than there are political benefits in claiming them. The changing economy and the changing society have moved local politics to a form of new and assertive politics which can no longer be constrained within the routines of the committee system. Much that has been accepted is now challenged.

The necessity for direct public provision of services is no longer accepted as of right. Professional definitions of need are widely challenged. The attack on institutional discrimination against ethnic minorities or against women exposes the values underlying existing practice. Constraint and cutback at a time of societal change force choice and challenge past values. Far from eschewing choice and hiding value issues, the new politics is confronting them.

Value choice is never a simple matter of choosing between conflicting values. In any action by the local authority many value issues are involved. The local authority is engaged in the work of balancing values. Choice does not lie between good and bad, or even between one good and another good. It is a choice between relative amounts of good and bad. The location of a new housing development can bring benefits to some and costs to others. Thus it is not helpful to focus the policy planning process upon separate objectives, as if the local authority faced an absolute choice between one objective and another and between activities that contribute to single objectives. In many a rural area the local authority seeks conservation and economic development. The real issue is not the objectives, but the balance between them. A local authority should be helped to seek desired balances or perhaps to avoid undesired balances. A budget is an exercise not in achieving particular objectives, but in balance between them or in avoiding imbalance.

It may be easier for councillors to be specific about what they wish to avoid than what they want to achieve. The political process can react to abuses in the present more easily than to ideals in the future. It is always easier to determine the wrong than the right. It is easier to identify the failure of past policies for the inner city than to identify the right policy.

Policy processes must recognise that in any pattern of services, many different values are involved. To expose the different values, activities have to be looked at from different and differing perspectives:

• how they affect different sectors of society;
• the choice between public goods and private goods;
• whether activities discriminate in impact, if not in intention, against particular groups.

On all these issues choice can lie hidden.

The local authority is and always will be constrained in its use of resources in relation to the needs and problems it faces. Until rate-capping, all local authorities had a choice on their level of resources, i.e. on the amount which they raise in taxes for expenditure on their services. A local authority also has a choice on how those resources are distributed. That choice is normally seen as a choice between activities or services. For rate-capped authorities the first choice, which is in effect the choice between public services and private expenditure, is eliminated. The second choice remains.

'The multi-valued choice' is at the heart of local government.

Multiple criteria of success are inherent in the government of any political or social unit, however small. For the multiple needs and diverse standards of expectation of people bring together in a place, interact with and limit each other in ways which cannot be ignored. Functional organisation can ignore problems which they set for each other; and when in doubt they can simplify their choices by referring to their function as defining their primary responsibility. But general organisations, even the smallest, have no built-in priorities to guide them in their multi-valued choices. They must decide not only what to do but what to want – more exactly what to value most in the concrete situation of every decision. They must define and redefine the unacceptable, not in one dimension alone but in many.

(Vickers, 1972, p. 134)

The local authority is not a single-purpose organisation, but a multi-purpose organisation. As the local government for an area, it is a general organisation 'with no built-in priorities to guide' in the multi-valued choice. The multi-valued choice is the choice between the many purposes of the authority, and is at heart of its budgetary process. The multi-valued choice is not choice about how to achieve, but about what to value.

The choice is made in the budgetary process. The budgetary process is a bargaining process. The new management will not turn resource allocation into a process that eliminates bargaining. But bargaining takes place within a structure of procedures which set conditions. The new management is concerned with the conditions of the bargaining process.

The bargaining processes in many authorities are structured by the continuing requirements of service provision. The traditional budget focused on the means by which activities are carried out with separate heads under each activity for 'employees', 'premises', 'supplies and services', etc.

The main actors involved have until recently been the treasurer, the chair of finance and service chairs and chief officers. A perspective on the role of local authorities as local government is not easily established by organisational interests focusing on finance alone or on the requirements of particular services. The corporate movement has built new organisational interests into the bargaining process in the roles of chief executive and chair of policy and resources. New organisational interests change the conditions of the bargaining processes, but new procedures and information are also required.

Budgets should reflect the political nature of choice. They can show the limits of choice, both in the short term and in the long term, the constraints on change and the extent to which they can be overcome by time. They can expose assumptions about standards and needs on which existing activities are based. The allocation of resources can be presented in ways that differ from the allocation of resources to meet the continuing requirements of services.

The presentation should take account of political requirements. Thus it can be politically meaningful to ask:

- How are resources distributed between different geographical areas?
- How are resources distributed between different social groups?
- How far are the resources of the authority directed at countering the effects of poverty, countering unemployment, or other policy priorities of the authority?
- How far does the allocation of resources conform to the manifesto of the majority party or to the differing manifestos of the parties in a hung authority?

Such information cannot be presented with the same precision as can the traditional budget, nor is it needed with the same precision to guide policy choice. The traditional budget was and is still in many local authorities a control document, not a document to support local choice.

Policy processes for the new management should provide a counter-information service on the use of resources to that developed for traditional management. The new management does not remove the bargaining process, nor should it. It does, however, change the conditions under which bargaining takes place.

## THE LONGER-TERM HORIZON OF CHOICE

An operational perspective focuses on the short term in which choice is limited. Many policies can only be achieved if pursued over the long term. Schools cannot be reorganised, policies of economic development established, new working practices negotiated with trade unions, or racial discrimination countered, if the horizon of concern is limited to a year.

'In any annual budget choice is limited to the margin', but choice can be extended over a longer time horizon. To limit the horizon of concern to the time-span of the annual budget is to cut short the political agenda. Significant change can take time, small changes can, by jointed incrementalism, lead over a longer period to major change. If different percentage increases are allocated each year to departments, the balance of resource allocation is changed very significantly over time. 'Give me an increment of growth and I will change the world, without anyone knowing it.' Jointed incrementalism requires policy guidelines over the longer term for sureness of cumulative impact.

Unless the longer term is recognised, choice is distorted. Some choices made in a particular year affect only that year, but other choices have impacts in years to come, increasing over time. Present choice can pre-empt future choice, and if the time horizon of concern is limited, that future choice will not have been considered.

Thus a decision on a capital programme may not have its full impact for several years to come. Yet that decision can pre-empt revenue resources in future years. Unless possible alternative use of revenue resources are considered alongside the capital programme, local choice is being determined, not by the political processes, but by the timing of decisions.

To consider the long term involves not merely resources, but the changing nature of society. Many decisions taken now have their impact in the future. They are justified not merely by their immediate but by their longer-term impact. Many training decisions as well as capital decisions would not be justified unless it is assumed that they will be as relevant in the future as in the present, but that again requires consideration of the longer term. Not to consider the longer term does not avoid prediction. It is to predict that the future will be like the present. Before the oil crisis energy use and petrol consumption were projected to continue upwards. Events can disturb the apparently safest projection.

Only by considering the longer term can choices be increased, distortion of choice be avoided and the future relevance of present decisions be considered. Policy processes should project the financial position beyond the one year horizon of the annual revenue budget. It will be argued that given the uncertainties of government grant, such projections are unrealistic. It is true that changes in the amount of grant, and even more in the rules governing grant, have introduced new uncertainties and new difficulties in longer term resource projection. However, a number of local authorities have shown the practicality of longer term financial planning. In Cambridgeshire a three year medium term financial plan is an established element in policy planning. Nor is Cambridgeshire alone. In 14 per cent of local authorities surveyed by the Audit Commission, current expenditure plans covering three years were prepared (Audit Commission, 1984b). To project revenue is not to produce a completely accurate projection. A projection can expose the likely range of possibilities. Not to make a projection involves more dangers than to make an inaccurate projection within understood limits.

Policy processes must also project the possibilities of societal change, based on the learning and the analysis of learning. *The Changing Face of Bradford* provides one example described in Chapter 5. In Cambridgeshire, as part of the preparation of a corporate ten year strategy, scenarios have been prepared giving 'a view of the future. Sometimes alternatives are shown so as not to give a false picture of certainty. Part of the report is written from the viewpoint of an observer in 1995 and the rest gives important background and assumptions from the 1985 situation' (Cambridgeshire 1985a). The scenarios are used to suggest issues that need to be confronted in the present and on which political guidelines are required.

Give high priority to economic development?

Continue preparation of social and community support services for a decade of increased demands from disadvantaged groups, and declining public sector resources? Anticipate a changed climate of attitudes to formal employment and unemployment, in which concern changes, part time jobs, and periods of independent activity will increase?

Develop new approaches to resource economy and generation in anticipation of further reductions in central government grant?

Develop the breakerage role of the County Council for the co-ordination and effective planning of related services?

Demonstrate that the County Council is an effective and accountable provider of services and help to restore the reputation of local government by example?

(Cambridgeshire, 1985a)

In the future much is possible. The future cannot be projected with certainty, yet not to explore the future is to assume that certainty can be found in the present.

## OUTWARD TOWARDS THE ENVIRONMENT

As local government, a local authority has to look beyond the services provided towards the problems felt and the opportunities perceived in the community. An operational perspective necessarily focuses on the services provided. Policy processes should give the local authority an alternative perspective that looks outward towards the environment.

⋅ If the local authority looks outward to the community, it will be able to judge its services, not by the activity undertaken, but by the extent to which the services meet problems seen and felt in the community. From an operational perspective, a service is justified by the activity undertaken. Performance measurement for operational management then becomes merely a way of measuring the level of that activity, as when the library service is measured by indicators of book provision. The National Consumer Council has suggested that to evaluate the service to the public there may be a need for performance measures that reach out beyond the organisation towards the consumer.

1. Performance measurement must be set within the political context of defining policies and setting objectives.
2. Measurement should attempt to relate service provision and quality to consumer and/or community preferences or needs, recognising that giving priority to certain needs remains a political activity.
3. To assess the effects of a service on consumers, one must start by asking which aspects of the service actually matter to them.
4. Services' consumer performance may be evaluated in a number of ways: through the use of performance indicators; surveys (whether carried out by local authorities or others); complaints; and 'soft information' from councillors' surgeries, HMI inspections of schools, professional self-evaluation and so on. All are valuable, and authorities should beware of giving undue weight to quantitative rather than qualitative measures.
5. Performance indicators – or numbers used to demonstrate aspects of performance – mean little on their own. They should generally be used to demonstrate relationships (for example, pupil–teacher ratios or the number of nursery school places in relation to the number of children in the area belonging to the relevant age group); to show trends; or to make comparisons, either within or between authorities.
6. Surveys may be necessary to determine consumer and community requirements, and to assess satisfaction with services, especially those aspects of service (such as quality) which are not easily quantified.
7. The number and nature of complaints can be used to assess satisfaction with services, even if imperfectly. Local authorities should take a more positive view of complaints and feed information about complaints into the process of performance planning and review.
8. If performance measurement is to work, it will need the support of key council members and officials. It will also need to be firmly established as part of an authority's system for reviewing needs/requirements, setting political objectives, monitoring performance, reviewing objectives, and reporting on performance.

9. Attention must be given to the public reporting of performance information, and the different information needs of
councillors, service managers, the public and so on.

10. In summary, local authorities should be more willing to
adopt a marketing approach to the provision of services. This
will entail a more rigorous examination of what people want,
and a greater determination to sell themselves to the public,
by demonstrating both what they can offer and what they
have achieved.

(National Consumer Council, 1983, pp. 6–7)

Looking outward to the community provides a basis for judging
present services and the need for change in those services. If the local
authority looks outward to the community, it will also identify problems to which its services might contribute, even though the problem
was not one at which the service was specifically directed. The need
will not, however, be recognised if the focus is on the service. Crime
prevention can easily be regarded as an issue for the police alone. If it
is regarded as an issue for the local authority, many steps can be taken
and not merely by the education and social services.

Physical steps can be taken by the local authority itself. For
example, it is widely known that street lighting reduces crime.
How often, though, does a local authority introduce street
lighting solely to reduce crime in an affected area? Much local
authority urban design has facilitated crime: subways are widely
feared and pedestrian precincts often hamper effective policing
and supervision. A cross-precinct bus route might be welcomed
not only by the public transport operator but also by the police.
Pedestrian movement can be better designed so as to reduce their
vulnerability to vandalism. Housing allocation policies can be
very influential in influencing crime patterns. There can be better
co-operation with the agencies concerned and with juvenile
delinquency in both the statutory and the voluntary sectors.

(Brooke, 1983, p. 11)

If the local authority looks outward to the community, it will
identify problems that are not adequately met by its services or by
those of other agencies. It will see opportunities that could be
realised by itself or by other agencies. These problems may require
or these opportunities invite either action or influence by the local
authority. Neither problem or opportunity will be seen by an
authority from an operational perspective. A report prepared for
Wolverhampton on the problem of youth unemployment illustrates
the possibilities:

A wider and more integrated approach to the social condition of youth unemployment could attempt a strategic intervention which attempts, not only to mitigate the worst effects of change within a given framework, but also to manage a process of change through adaptation of the institutions at the local state which are under local control and in a way that maximises the autonomies and powers of those unduly affected by change. This means adopting a stated policy on youth as an operational priority in all main departments, and the development of a central institutional framework capable of grasping the situation of the unemployed, and the full range of their needs, and empowered to respond to those needs in a co-ordinated and integrated way. There needs to be a decisive move on from leisure and social provision to address under areas including: livelihood; welfare rights; employment opportunities; counselling; housing; social services provision; post YTS, educational and training opportunities; access to building and resources; the need for young people to define their own problems and needs and to be involved in the running of services aimed at meeting them; the necessity of political, economic and social advocacy for youth and its sub-sections. The provision of leisure, recreation and cultural activities is important, of course, but the opportunities will not be taken-up anyway by wide sections of the youth population unless they are located in a general social and political programme linking many sites and provision through information and networking and addressed to the promotion of an overall philosophy of the emancipation of youth and the development of their rights. The LA, on some part of it, must be seen to be 'on the side' of the young people.

(Wolverhampton, 1985, p. 219)

Policy processes must reach outward to the community. The learning local authority does just that, but the learning processes must feed into policy processes, which should enforce the required pause for reflection on the learning. The policy processes protect learning and responding to what is learnt, but they must also protect choice in direction. Learning and responding alone is not government. Responding does not involve choice of direction but assumes the direction is correct, although the actual route followed may have to vary. Learning and response and choice in direction have to be brought together in the policy processes.

## A NETWORK OF GOVERNMENT

The local authority is one public agency amongst many. Those agencies are taken account of by traditional management, when required for the routines of service provision as in the co-operation between health authorities and local authorities in school health inspections.

A local authority as local government is concerned not merely with its own activities, but with those of other agencies. Problems and issues do not divide neatly into the responsibilities of the various agencies. The care of the aged is the concern of shire districts, of shire counties, and of health authorities, as well as of the Department of Health and Social Security. Issues and problems can be lost between boundaries that divide the system of government. It is difficult to locate responsibility and concern for rural and urban deprivation, for the local economy or for the impact of unemployment.

In an era of resource constraint, the fragmentation of resources is a barrier to their effective use. The separate agencies recruit their own skills, maintain their own information stocks, have land, property and equipment held for their own purposes – all of which could be more fully utilised if available to other agencies of government.

The developing politics of local government extends beyond the organisational boundaries of the local authorities. The local authority no longer ignores the role played by its councillor representatives on health authorities or other agencies.

The new management looks beyond the activities of the authority. The management of influence is required as well as the management of action.

In Thamesdown, the local authority has produced *A New Vision for Thamesdown*. This is a consultation document setting out the 'Choices for the Nineties' for Thamesdown, a district council in Wiltshire, based largely on Swindon. In the analysis importance is laid on the operating environment:

> A great many outside organisations and influences impinge on the work of the Borough Council and, for convenience, these are described collectively as the 'operating environment'. It is clear from the foregoing parts of this report that, whilst the area could not have developed as it has without the support of some elements of the operating environment, others may be hostile and all are sometimes uncertain. The ability to manage the support and the uncertainty has been one of the most valuable attributes of the Borough Council and is one which will be even more important in the future, whatever policy is adopted.
>
> (Thamesdown, 1984, p. 14)

The Report goes on to argue:

> It was noted earlier that many powers and services essential to the fulfilment of Borough Council policy are outside its direct control.

Equally the Council itself cannot generate more than a fraction of the investment and employment that the area needs. Limited resources will inevitably mean less direct control so it will be essential to build up the advocacy role in order to gain the trust and confidence of other service agencies, the Government, business and the general public in furthering Council aims. Given the possible continuation of a challenging and, in some respects, adverse environment the advocacy role will be more vital in the late 1980's and 1990's than it has ever been.

(Thamesdown, 1984, p. 34)

To exercise influence or to undertake advocacy information is required. Policy processes should ensure that within the local authority there is as full information as possible upon the policies and resources of other public agencies. A special budget could show not merely the local authority's resources but the range of public resources in its area, possibly on a client basis, as developed by Howard Glennerster for the elderly in Wandsworth covering both NHS and local government expenditure (Glennerster, 1983, p. 27).

A published community assessment such as *The Changing Face of Bradford* can stimulate public debate of the problems facing the area. In the light of such an analysis a local authority can set priorities not merely for its own services but for the management of influence. Such policy processes reflect the governmental role of local authorities.

## AN AWARENESS OF UNCERTAINTY

'Planning is an ideal, but in an uncertain world it is unrealistic.' With such phrases, local authorities retreat to the routines of service provision. They retreat from an awareness of uncertainty to the apparent certainty of service provision.

Uncertainty does not destroy the case for policy processes although it removes the case for forms of policy planning that assume certainty in a comprehensive plan. A failure to plan does not avoid assumptions about the future. It is, again, to assume that the future will be like the present.

The problems faced by a local authority can change beyond and above predictions. Past population projections and energy assumptions have been disproved by events. Knowledge and available technologies can change in ways that were unanticipated. The local authority has moved from the apparent certainties of the long years of growth to cutback in resources, new interventions by central government and seemingly endless changes in the rules governing local government finance. The political process itself is changing in ways that cannot be fully anticipated. There can be no certainty in government. There can only be eddies of relative certainty and uncertainty.

Traditional management imposes its own certainties by routinising experience and reaction. Change can breach those certainties and bring crisis. Policy processes for the new management can take account of uncertainty in ways that are impossible for traditional management, because it is not tied to the certainty of existing service provision.

Policy processes should recognise uncertainty as a factor to be allowed for. Policy processes can seek to predict not merely in trend projection, but in projecting where trends will build counter-trends or where the qualitatively different is developing. In prediction, eddies of relative certainty and uncertainty can be plotted.

Flexibility can be built into the policy processes themselves. The mistake lies in the fixed policy plan, not in policy processes. The corporate plan specifying each activity in detail for succeeding years assumed the certainties of service provision rather than the uncertainties of the environment. The certain plan has no means of meeting unanticipated change. Many such a plan was destroyed in the ending of the growth in expenditure which they assumed.

Policy processes should allow for a range of possibilities. Thus alternative resource can be allowed for, covering different possible grant settlements from central government. A worst-case grant projection can be set out (and even that involves certain assumptions) with choices as to how more favourable settlements can be responded to. There would be not one plan but a range of possibilities.

## SELECTIVITY IN POLICY PLANNING

The comprehensive plan detailing each activity and the plans for that activity with an undifferentiated certainty is a plan doomed to failure. Any unanticipated change destroys or distorts the plan. In particular such a plan cannot cope with growth or cutback. It gives no guide between what is important and unimporant. For that, selectivity is necessary.

Selectivity is, however, not an unfortunate necessity imposed by uncertainty. Selectivity is at the heart of the policy processes for direction and choice. Policy processes have to select from the complex environment significant demands and significant changes and to identify where in the activities of the authority major change is required, and emphasis and protection needed. From the undifferentiated policy processes should differentiate out those issues which cannot be dealt with by the procedures of traditional management.

Policy processes can provide focus and direction by selectivity. The comprehensive plan that states all gives neither direction nor guidance. Such a plan is easily prepared: few choices have to be made; few priorities have to be given; little understanding is required. A comprehensive plan is, however, as unhelpful as it is easily prepared. Selectivity is the hard task, because it involves choice.

Selectivity is guided politically in identifying priority areas for change and for protection. The manifesto is a guide – although it too may lose direction in comprehensive detail. Selectivity can focus on change in the balance of activities, identifying key areas for growth or decline, bringing together environmental change and political choice – learning and direction.

Selectivity can focus on the strategic. There has been a tendency in local government to assume a necessary connection between strategy and geographical scale. It has come to be synonymous with 'metropolitan' or 'regional'. If one regards a strategy as 'an appropriate response to a policy problem which involves the (complex) interaction of a number of distinct elements, which are inter-related in such a way that the treatment of the elements in isolation from one another may be insufficient to cope with the problem . . .' (Leach and Stewart, 1984), then it does not necessarily involve the large-scale. A strategic issue is one that has widespread ramifications, and involves interconnections between many events and functions – the impact of unemployment is for many a local authority, such an issue. A strategy 'will involve the specification of appropriate policy guidelines (or framework, or parameters) specific enough to influence action/decisions, but stopping at an appropriate level of detail below which decisions can sensibly be left to a "non-strategic" decision-making process' (Leach and Stewart, 1984).

Selectivity, however determined, ensures focus and focus is likely to aid achievement. Absence of selectivity in comprehensive planning is a declaration that everything matters, which means that nothing matters. Selectivity is a declaration of what matters.

Selectivity underlies the Cambridgeshire Medium Term Planning system which

> is a necessary discipline in the overall management of the Authority. It focuses attention on its main strategic aims, considers how to deal with the national and locally determined constraints

on expenditure, and attempts to ensure that services are efficiently provided to meet the County's needs. It directs resources in a systematic manner to meet changing priorities, and changes in the geographical location and age structure of the population. The merits of new schemes are assessed in the light of overall objectives before scarce resources are allocated to them. The system enables the Council's plans to be co-ordinated with those of District Councils and other public bodies to promote joint working.

(Cambridgeshire, 1984)

Guidelines are laid down, not on a comprehensive basis, but selectively identifying the priorities of the council. In the 1985 medium-term guidelines, these included services for frail elderly people, young children and their families, unemployed people and the prevention of crime (Cambridgeshire, 1985b). As political control changes so in Cambridgeshire may the priorities change.

## A SENSE OF DIRECTION

In the day-to-day activities of any organisation a sense of direction can be lost. For local government, direction is required. The products of the policy processes should give a sense of direction to staff. Amongst those products must be statements to which those in the authority can relate and against which they can judge particular actions.

No sense of direction is given by a detailed corporate plan, setting out each activity in detail. Direction is lost in the detail. One does not show a way through a wood by showing the position of every tree.

Initiative is lost in over-specification. If a local authority seeks an entrepreneurial approach, it wishes opportunities to be seized, not neglected 'because they are not in the plan'. The local authority entrepreneurs need directions but they do not need all the details of the route.

The local authority needs above all to make clear to the staff the values that guide its policies and should guide the activities of the authority. Wrekin District Council has identified as its key values Quality, Caring and Fairness (Paine, 1985).

These values have, however, to be translated into activities. This is in part the function of the new management, showing the importance of the new values in action. In the Wrekin District Council as described by the chief executive:

We decided against the 'big bang' approach of formally presenting and publicising the values through the whole organisation,
which could have led to the whole exercise being discredited as a
gimmick. Instead, and apart from the action stated above, the
Chief Officers and myself resolved to take the lead and attempt to
inculcate and develop the values by personal example. Thus, we
take every possible opportunity to reinforce the values and apply
them to existing and developing services. We do this by means of,
at the one end of the scale, a simple thank you for a job well done
which reflects one or more of the values to, at the other end, a
positive measure to enhance (say) the quality of a particular
service. Thus by influencing the values through the people in the
organisation and in direct service delivery, we hope the overall
level of services and the commitment of the people who carry
them out will reach new heights.

Where do we go from here? Well, it would be foolish to pretend
that the whole organisation is throbbing with the words
QUALITY, CARE and FAIRNESS. We've still got a lot of work to
do to ensure that the values are communicated and upheld
throughout the organisation. We accept that it's a task which will
not be completed overnight. After all, the best and most successful
organisations have built up their culture over many years. But
through our new employees who are being increasingly 'brought
up' on the values, through our existing employees who are
gradually acknowledging the values and through a continuous
review of services in terms of the values, the cumulative effects are
beginning to be noticed.

We need to do much more work on examining our services and
attempting to match them up with the values. We need to find
more ways of reinforcing the values with our existing employees
and gaining their commitment to them. We need to recognise
more fully positive responses to the values (perhaps by a system of
non-financial rewards) to identify and deal with negative
responses. It should be made quite clear throughout the organisation that employees who display the values will stand a far
better chance of 'getting on' in the broadest sense than those who
scorn them. We should give discreet groups of employees (e.g.
Cyclic Maintenance Team, Typing Pool) the responsibility of
looking at the values in their own service area and the responsibility for implementing any changes in practices after agreement
with their manager (i.e. akin to the Quality Circle approach).

We intend to ask new starters what their impressions are of our
values after a few months. We want to ask a cross-section of the
public at periodic intervals how their perception of Council

services matches our values – because in time our values and the public image ought to be one. We should send employees to and from organisations where we know our kind of values are displayed in an exemplary manner.

(Paine, 1985)

It is helpful if the policy processes go on from the values to show how they can guide policy. There can be no standard format for documents giving direction. Attempts to describe the multi-dimensioned activities of local authorities under standard headings of Needs, Problems, Objectives, Activity, Input and Output is to reduce rich information to the structure of a form. It is an exercise in classification, not in showing direction, and remains unreadable and unread.

Documents to give direction are not programmes. They are designed more to be what the Audit Commission has described as:

Vision: What the authority is seeking to be or achieve.

(Audit Commission, 1984, p. 5)

The language is looser. Direction is given rather than over-specification. The document prepared as *A New Vision for Thamesdown* is an example:

In general it was agreed that there should be some continued growth of the area to meet the needs generated by earlier migration but considerable emphasis was placed on achieving a satisfactory balance between new development and the needs and problems of existing settlements and communities. Such a balance would have to recognise the renewal of older areas and facilities, intervention in development to meet shortcomings in private sector provision and the enhancement of the quality of life throughout the Borough. Great importance was attached to securing high environmental standards and a full range of social infrastructure to meeting the needs of disadvantaged minorities. It was accepted that the rate and scale of development might need to be controlled carefully by various means in order to achieve those aims and to avoid undue pressure on restricted public resources and facilities.

(Thamesdown, 1984, p. 5)

Within this strategy, four approaches to the council's role were considered. The favoured approach was selective intervention in any future development, leaving the rest to private enterprise, to be controlled through the planning system:

Such an approach would still allow the Council to exert some direct control over future growth and would help to ensure that adequate social infrastructure is provided in new development. At the same time, it should also permit the retention of resources to deal with needs and problems anywhere in Thamesdown that are within its powers and are not being met by any other agency. If this process of selective intervention is pursued consistently in the period up to the 1990's, it will not only represent a modification of Council policy in recognition of changing conditions but should also offer a wider choice of action. Alongside the acceptance of the preferred approach there was a firm determination to maintain and, where necessary, intensify a strong advocacy and lobbying role on behalf of Thamesdown and its residents, businesses and workers.

(Thamesdown, 1984, pp. 5–6)

This is a document that starts from Thamesdown as local government, concerned with its area and with the activities of other agencies, involved in the management of influence as of action, and above all with choice and with maintaining room for choice.

An agreed and accepted vision of the kind of overall community we are seeking to achieve is vitally necessary both to motivate the Council's organisation and to enlist the support of many interests. Moreover such a vision is already emerging. In addition to pursuing the broad concepts of a thriving local economy, a caring and participating community and an attractive environment, that new vision embodies the idea of the Council giving a clear lead but also acting as referee between many conflicting interests. As such, the vision includes those aspects of Council activity that will give it effect as far as powers and resources will permit, notably intervening in development and renewal in specific rather than general ways, improving and extending services where necessary or at least maintaining them, identifying and tackling problems that no other agency can deal with and pursuing other agencies for the service on inputs that they should be providing.

To establish its credibility a new vision should imply, and could state the assumptions that it will remain valid for some time to come and can, therefore, be sustained, that the whole of the Council's organisation will be geared to supporting it, that if necessary it can be sustained with no significant real increase in resources and that it is based explicitly on an ultimate limit of development and on the permanent protection of the most important features of landscape and built environment. Furthermore, the vision should not be tied to a specific time for its achievement.

The report referred earlier to the 'style' of Council activity: that style should depend on and emerge from the vision and should create a consistency of purpose that all are aware of. It needs to reiterate a spirit of impartial public service in which leadership, encouragement and support are the key factors.

(Thamesdown, 1984, p. 58)

## A PROTECTED PAUSE

Service provision knows no pause. It creates its own necessity. Action has to be taken continuously to ensure services are provided. There is an urgency and an immediacy in the requirements of an operational perspective.

Policy processes need organisational protection if they are to be established, and even more if they are to be maintained, because of the necessary dominance of service provision in the working of the local authority. Policy processes require an organisational pause. Organisational time and space have to be protected against the pressures of operational timetables.

Separate policy processes are required. By creating a setting or a period protected from the pressures of service provision, opportunity is provided to reconsider the need for many activities that appear so necessary in the day-to-day working of the authority. By changing the rhythm of the organisation – if only in a limited way – the conditions for organisational thinking are changed.

Organisational time and space are protected by procedures. A procedure is needed to enforce a pause in the procedures of traditional management. Only if policy processes are written into the timetable of action will they have the same urgency as the requirements of service provision.

A system is needed to counter a system. The dilemma is that the new system can cease to challenge, once established. By writing policy processes into the procedures of the authority, determining when and how choices are presented or strategy is approved, the danger is that what are intended to challenge routines become themselves routines. Policy processes can become merely cumbersome procedures justifying themselves in the paper produced.

Yet procedures are required to protect a policy perspective. They can bring a different character and dynamism to the working of the organisation. Meetings that focus on policy processes should be different in form, and even in settings, from meetings required for operational management. Management team and policy and resources committees can occasionally escape from the committee room. The committee table itself implies a particular way of doing business. The rules of the game have to be changed and be seen to have changed.

The one- or two-day seminar at which the council leadership and chief officers consider the main issues facing the authority without the pressure of an agenda or decision can be built into the council diary – that imperative of organisational time.

In Devon a 'Policy Debate' was instituted in 1981 for the then Conservative administration based on an analysis of:

a)   The major influences in the social, economic and institutional framework of the County to which the various services would need to respond; and

b)   How in fact the services should respond to these influences.
(Macklin, 1983, p. 84)

These were described as Devon Trends and 'The Policy Choices'. The Policy Debate took place at Dartington Hall and has been described by the chief executive:

> After discussion with the Council Leader, it was decided to involve initially the Committee Chairman only (about 13 Councillors) and to hold a 24 hour session away from County Hall.
>
>   It did not take us long to select the venue, as we are fortunate enough to have Dartington Hall and College on our 'patch', and to my mind one could scarcely find a more suitable meeting place than this secluded and graceful estate, with its 14th Century Hall and manicured lawns and hedges. It gave us at once at atmosphere of studiousness and comfort, neither of which qualities are readily apparent in our too-familiar committee rooms in Exeter.
>
>   The plan for the policy debate session was to start (after a short introduction by me) with the Chief Officers briefly commenting on their respective sections in the booklet, highlighting the main issues and pointing out where the members' decisions were required. In the evening, Mr. William Plowden, Director of the RIPA, was to give what turned out to be a fascinating and significant view of public policy making – we had invited Mr. Plowden to act as catalyst and to help us to draw together some of the main strands of the debate – which certainly heightened both Members' and Officers' enthusiasm for the whole event.
>
>   The final session on the next morning was to belong to the members, where they would give their own views on the service priorities to be followed up to 1985/86, and hopefully lay down some guidelines for us to follow during that period.
>
>   In retrospect I regard initiation of the policy debate as a success, although at the end of the session just described it was clear that

we would need to hold a mark II to add flesh to some of the bones which had been (dare I say) unearthed. Some quite firm conclusions were in fact reached, for example the Chairmen's evident desire to enhance provision of social services, and a number of areas were delineated for immediate research to be carried out. Important in this category was an examination of various aspects of the 'rural' question which is so important in Devon – are children from small rural primary schools educationally disadvantaged during their time in the secondary sector? And how has the reduction in rural bus services *really* affected the inhabitants of the County's remoter areas?

Work has started on these and other topics, as one cannot make good policies with a less than complete understanding of the problems one is setting out to solve.

(Macklin, 1983, pp. 85–6)

Such meetings break the working pattern set by the operational perspective and protect the working pattern required for a policy perspective.

A local authority may see as part of its policy processes any or all of the following procedures:

(1)   A local authority may seek to establish a three to five year revenue projection and a broad plan for expenditure related to that projection, against which particular activities may be judged.

(2)   A local authority may institute an annual review procedure by both the policy and resources committee and by each service committee. This review would include both the service view and the corporate view on the changing environment. Each committee would be asked for an assessment of emerging problems and issues, key strengths and weaknesses, and an assessment of past achievement. Discussed outside the normal committee cycle a policy perspective is enforced.

(3)   A local authority could carry out an agreed programme of policy analyses into topic areas.

(4)   A local authority could institute manifesto implementation and review procedures, involving a timetabled series of reports into how far the manifesto has been carried out, and where and how obstacles can be overcome.

(5)   The local authority might require policy statements and reviews from, and for, all its representatives on outside bodies.

(6)   A local authority could prepare resource analyses as background to the budgetary processes showing the redistributive

effect of the budgetary provision between different areas and social groups.

(7) A local authority could prepare a policy statement indicating the key choices made by the local authority so that it could guide staff.

These are but possibilities from many possibilities. They are no prescription, but merely an indication of some ways ideas can be caught in procedures. Each of these procedures brings into the working of the organisation a perspective that would not otherwise be present. The aim is to write new attitudes into the working which can influence practice.

One does not achieve a new perspective by procedures alone, yet procedures may be needed to enforce the perspective. One does not achieve a new perspective by organisation alone, yet organisation may be needed to reinforce the perspective. One does not achieve a new perspective by changing culture alone, yet changing culture may be needed to reinforce the perspective. In the end, attitude and ideas are what matters.

- In the routines of traditional management, the outside world is reduced to the scale of the organisation, and in that reduction much is lost. That is where learning has to start.
- Every organisation has to make the assumptions necessary to carry out its operations. Local authorities as local government start from a challenge to those assumptions.
- An operational perspective is necessary. That is why local government needs protection in policy processes.
- To learning and challenge have to be added direction.
- Politics should give direction in local government, but it can be lost in the committee agenda. One can, however, start again from the manifesto.
- Choice can be hidden in the necessity of present activity, but to accept that necessity is to make a choice. A budget can express that choice, or it can avoid it.
- If one only looks a year ahead, one will never break out of constraints on action and on thought. As the time-horizon extends, so choice increases.
- All local authorities forecast the future. It is merely a question of whether they see the future as beyond the present.
- The services can absorb attention. They justify by their existence, but problems remain to be met and opportunities to be sought out.
- A local authority can influence where it cannot act, but influence has to be managed as well as action.

- Uncertainty can be planned for, but not if the plan does not allow for it.
- The comprehensiveness of detail allows no room for choice; it is in selectivity that direction is given.
- An authority that sets no direction for its staff can hardly be surprised if they do not find the way.
- Procedures are needed to counter procedures; that is their importance and their danger.
- If an authority does not learn, it does not govern. Yet learning is not enough; there must be choice if direction is to be found.

# 8

# Creating Space for Responsiveness in Action

## FORMAL CONTROL

Policy has to be expressed in action. If policy is not translated into the activities required, it will not be implemented. Yet if the activities required are over-specified at the centre of the authority, implementation will be so constrained that there is no space for responsiveness in action, and the reality of rule-bound policy implementation may be very different from the hopes of policy intention. Control is required to ensure policy is translated into action, but control should leave space for responsiveness. Effective control ensures political purpose is achieved in responsiveness. Traditional management provides the form but not the reality of control.

The organising principles of hierarchy, uniformity and functionalism determine the conditions of management. They ensure that the authority is structured to provide uniform service to functionally defined standards, reinforced by hierarchical control. Political control emphasises rather than lessens that hierarchical control. The committee is the formal focus for the hierarchical control. That formal role gives legitimacy to the actions of staff within the authority.

The hierarchies of the authority fit the formal requirements of political control. They are designed to ensure that decisions of the committee are translated into action. Decisions of the committee are translated into rules and into procedures to enforce them. Exceptions to the rules, or decisions above a specified limit, have to be reinforced to committees, and the agendas become filled with the detailed decisions required.

The norms of public accountability reinforce the tendency to detailed control. The norms limit discretion and encourage the specification of rules and precise adherence to those rules. If a rule properly laid down is carried out, the local authority ombudsman will find no maladministration, even if the decision is regarded as unjust by all involved in it – the staff bound by the rules, the committee caught by past decisions, and the client-complainant. For public accountability is interpreted as rule-boundedness and the ombudsman is concerned with public accountability. Yet that detailed control is self-defeating. It neither ensures effective political control or effective management. It denies the possibility of responsiveness in action.

Detailed control weakens managerial responsibility. The passing upward of decisions, the prescription of rule and the preferred uniformities of practice have the effect of reducing the individual official's sense of responsibility. 'That is the committee's policy', 'The committee have decided', are natural responses, yet mean the passing of a responsibility to a committee, which probably never envisaged some of the consequences of the piece of paper, nodded through as the tenth item on a long-forgotten agenda.

Managerial capacity is weakened by lack of room for manoeuvre. If managerial action is over-determined by hierarchical control, then there is little room for managerial initiative. Management becomes less important than rule-adherence or, in its absence, good professional practice, which can sometimes enforce over-conformity even more subtly and more dangerously. Responsiveness becomes rule-breaking because there is no space left for management action.

The committee of a local authority will have its budget approved by the council. In traditional management that budget will specify not merely the overall amount of resources or its allocation to main activities, but also the way those resources will be used. Expenditure will be allocated to such categories as staff, purchase of goods, fuel costs, and transport. Financial control ensures that operational units keep not merely within their overall budgetary allocation but within the allocation to particular categories. At the same time separate controls apply to the manpower establishment of the unit, and separate procedures govern changes in that establishment, or the filling of vacant posts within the approved establishment, even though there is room within the expenditure allocated in the budget for that post to be filled.

There are procedures to vire expenditure from one budgetary head to another. Those procedures often require approval within the hierarchy and special submissions to committees. They define the movement of resources between budgetary heads as an exceptional act requiring justification.

This system of control emphasises adherence to prescribed allocation rather than management responsibility for the effective use of resources. Officers become dependent on the decisions of others and can pass the blame accordingly. They come to see their task as bidding for resources rather than deploying the resources available to maximise impact.

Such financial and other controls are justified as necessary to ensure the proper use of public resources. As financial constraint has grown, financial controls and establishment controls have tightened. At first sight, that seems the natural reaction. In a crisis the immediate response is centralisation. Yet it can be a self-defeating response. Detailed centralised control does not necessarily ensure the effective use of resources that it is designed to achieve. That effective use cannot be achieved by control at the centre, but only by those close to the use of those resources.

The argument is not against financial control. It is an argument against over-specification in control, as weakening rather than strengthening effective use of resources. Traditional management reinforces detailed control and in doing so weakens resource management.

Committees seek control in detail but fail to achieve it. So much information fills the agenda of committees in their attempt to control, that control is lost. Important merges with unimportant. As decision follows decision, there is the illusion of control far from the reality of action.

> Councillors cling with passion to every jot and title of the paraphernalia of what they delude themselves is 'control'. Delegation of authority over even trivial chores is regarded with profound suspicion, regardless of the fact that the workload nowadays is such as to defeat the most zealous of councillors. Any suggestion that the burden be shared with lay members of the public is apt to be regarded as the dereliction of duty. A firm grip is maintained on any proposal for the sharing of power to make decisions with community groups of any sort. The consequence is that though the system is operated efficiently enough, the sheer weight and volume of the agendas presented to members defeats the very purpose for which they were originally intended. The routine of committee meetings which go to make up a committee cycle has become self-defeating, itself a hindrance to the efficiency of the system of accountability, a cumbersome and time-consuming operation.
>
> (Simey, 1985, p. 27)

Yet committee members are using the only instrument they have been given – committee business – to control managerial action, which cannot be effectively controlled in this way, only frustrated by removing managerial responsibility.

Often the result is that frustrated political purpose seeks ever greater control. The outcome is a further weakening of management responsibility and less responsive management action, resulting in greater control or special *ad hoc* investigations which deny rather than advance management responsibility. The search for political control seems ever opposed to responsiveness in action. No other solution appears possible for traditional management with its emphasis on hierarchical control.

The new management does not have to accept the conditions of traditional management. In new conditions effective political control can be combined with effective management. Effective political control will not be achieved by controlling all, but by determining what requires to be controlled, leaving space for management responsibility and responsiveness in action.

## EFFECTIVE CONTROL

The new management should break away from detailed control, and should be based on effective control. Its guiding principles are political direction, but yet the avoidance of over-specification. To seek politically to determine all is to determine nothing. Only in political selectivity can direction be given in separating out the politically important from the trivial. Within a sense of direction there can be devolution of management responsibility.

Devolution of management responsibility is not the granting of total managerial discretion. It is a recognition that total control is ineffective, first because it over-burdens the controller and, second, because it assumes that the controller has all knowledge and all understanding. Total control breaks down under the burdens and under the unreality of the assumptions. Discretion will always exist because it is impossible to devise policies that fit every eventuality. By aiming at the achievable, effective control can be established.

The devolution of management responsibility is not justified merely by the impossibility of total control but is justified by the positive of releasing management initiative for responsiveness in action. Devolution provides the authority with the diversity that comes from innovation, and the learning that diversity brings.

The new management recognises that both management devolution and effective control are needed to achieve political purpose in reality as opposed to in the agendas of committees.

# A SCRUTINY OF CONTROL

A strategy of devolving management responsibility requires scrutiny of existing control systems, and of the role of the organisational hierarchies that support them.

- What would happen if the control did not exist?
- Would it matter?
- What is the real purpose of the control?

These questions probe the organisational gains from control. Other questions probe the costs:

- What are the financial (including staffing costs) of the control?
- Does the control make management initiative more difficult?
- If so, what sort of initiative does the control restrict?

Control has costs and benefits. In extreme cases the costs of control clearly outweigh any possible benefits. At one time local authority practice was to check every invoice, even though the cost of checking small invoices clearly outweighed any possibility of savings. This practice, long abandoned in most authorities, parodied the working of traditional management. It is not usually so clear-cut in financial terms. The real cost lies in the weakening of management responsibility and in reducing the responsiveness of the local authority.

Scrutiny should focus on the rules governing virement, and on establishment control duplicating financial control, as both restrict the freedom of a manager to deploy and redeploy resources in cost-effective ways.

Holtham and Palk have pointed out the need for greater flexibility in financial controls:

> The progressive approach to virement has a presumption in favour of the flexibility in the interests of service needs and economy of operation ... It is also our view that finance officers should now quite explicitly seek a reduction in the extent of detailed financial control from the central finance department, particularly in the fields of objective expenditure and income analysis, and to the delegation of these activities to cost centres, subject to adequate financial regulations. It may be questioned whether the detailed budget (e.g. planning department – books £100) is the most significant level for central control purposes. Firm but wide-ranging financial manpower controls should be the objective.
>
> (Holtham and Palk, 1981, pp. 39–40)

Holtham has gone on to argue:

> It is essential that cash and manpower controls are harmonised and do not duplicate each other. One of the effects of restraint has been a wide ranging analysis in some authorities of how the manpower control function should operate at a time when financial limits provide an overall framework in themselves. Some councils have reduced the central manpower control function in size and made service committees or chief officers primarily responsible for control within cash limits and establishments. Others are developing methods by which committees can be given greater flexibility in grading and numbers.
>
> (Holtham, 1981, p. 18)

Effective control replaces detailed control. Effective control ensures political direction but allows the devolution of management responsibility by requiring that:

- the organisational culture necessary for the new management pervades the organisation;
- each officer has an appreciation of the political purposes and of the policies pursued by the authority;
- each officer understands the scope of his or her responsibility;
- each officer understands what has to be achieved and the conditions which have to be observed;
- each officer has responsibility for the resources to carry out the task;
- each officer is encouraged to show responsiveness in action;
- each officer is held accountable for performance.

## VALUES ON POLITICAL PURPOSES

The devolution of management responsibility is only likely to support the new management if there is an organisational culture reinforcing its values. If the devolution of management responsibility takes place within a culture dominated by professionalism, the devolution will merely lead to further emphasis on professionalism, denying political will. That will not lead to effective control but to political frustration. Organisational values such as those suggested in Chapter 4 are the new management's precondition for the devolution of management responsibilities.

An emphasis on values lessens the need for detailed control. Values can guide management action more effectively than controls, for values permit flexibility. The manager applies the values and in that application can be responsive to community needs. The values of public service can help to build the community manager.

Beyond the continuing organisational values of the new management, managers must understand the political policies and purposes of the authority. For understanding requires not rules covering every eventuality but policies setting out what the authority is seeking to achieve – whether those policies are the long-established policies of the department carried forward under different party administrations or new policies adopted by an incoming administration. The policy message and its political content must be understood as part of the working conditions for the managers.

The new management of local authorities places value on the political process. Management in a local authority cannot, however, respond to the council's political purposes without communication of those purposes. Councillors assume that their policies must be understood by their staff. The staff often only know of the council's policies from isolated quotations in the local press. Unless the local authority devotes attention to ensuring that the policies of the majority party are understood, it is hardly surprising if they are not implemented in accordance with the intention.

Policies can be over-elaborated for understanding. Many a manifesto reads like a committee agenda in its detail, with possibly as much impact. That can be argued to be an improvement on the bland assurance of past manifestos that the party 'believes in education' but carries its own confusions. The need is for policy statements by political leadership, reinforced by meetings, by visits and by actions that emphasise key directions in terms meaningful for action, but do not over-specify action beyond the requirements of political purpose. These statements should not reiterate the known, listing activities being carried out by the authority, but should stress the new directions and highlight the important changes. A base must be laid for management understanding as a necessary condition of the devolution of management responsibility.

## RESPONSIBILITY CENTRES

Effective control is based on responsibility centres to which a budget is allocated and to which costs can be ascribed. These responsibility centres provide a basis for the devolution of management responsibility and the development of the community manager.

Some local authorities such as Cambridgeshire and Solihull have carried out pilot projects in making the school a responsibility centre, with what is described in Solihull as 'financial autonomy'

(Humphrey and Thomas, 1985, p. 419) by which is meant control over its own budget. Cambridgeshire County Council resolved in 1981 'that the Education Committee be asked to consider more flexibility in the control of their finances in 1982–83 by giving authority to the Governors of secondary schools to control their own budgets within a total cash limit as established by the Council's budget where the accountancy back-up is available from the Director of Finance and Administration; as a first stage the practice to be introduced in establishments where they have agreed to accept this responsibility' (Hinds, 1984). In both Cambridgeshire and Solihull the approach is being extended to other schools beyond the pilot project. East Sussex has a similar project for patch teams in Social Services. Other authorities such as Hammersmith and Fulham are establishing responsibility centres within the main departments of the authority.

Within a responsibility centre, the manager deploys the resources allocated in carrying out the required tasks. There can be constraints placed upon management and conditions to be met. Managers given responsibility may be required to ensure a specified standard of maintenance for the property under their control. They may be required to use certain services of the local authority, although the more constraints are put upon them, the greater difficulty there may be in the achievement of their tasks. It can be argued that the responsible manager should only be required to use central services if there are major advantages to the authority. Thus the Audit Commission in recommending central vehicle fleet management in local authorities also recommends that:

> User departments should have the ultimate sanction of being able to go outside the authority for their vehicles or maintenance if they can demonstrate that it would be consistently cheaper.
>
> (Audit Commission, 1984, p. 5)

Not all the conditions to be met relate to the use of resources. Conditions may express the general policies of the authority, such as its policy on race relations, and as such are less to be regarded as constraints but as part of the management task, fulfilling as they do the political purposes of the authority.

## ACCOUNTABLE MANAGEMENT

The devolution of management responsibility provides space for action, but control is ensured by accountability through the hierarchy that remains to committee and Council. The community managers must account for their performance. If this were not so, there would be ineffective rather than effective control. Accountable management is required, but its form should not be such that it becomes another form of detailed control.

Accountable management has been described as:

The management of expenditure, once budgets have been allocated, requires a more detailed specification of objectives and useful measures of performance wherever possible. Managers need to know how much they may spend: why they should spend it; and how their expenditure and results through the year compare with the plan. While the centre of the department receives regular information about the use of resources and the effectiveness of activities, individual managers can then be held accountable for their performance, and provided these conditions are met, can have more say in the composition of their budgets and greater freedom to manage within them. This delegation of authority should help them to improve the efficiency and effectiveness of their units, and to be more accountable for so doing.

(Financial Management in Government Departments, 1983, p. 2)

The Audit Commission has given examples of what accountable management could mean in local government:

Every senior manager would agree
1.   Three or four major tasks to be completed during the year (e.g. the delivery of a new service, or specified improvements in service standards).
2.   'Accountabilities' and their relative importance – those items for which officers can expect to be called to account.
3.   A specification under each 'accountability' of
     – performance goals;
     – the measure used to judge progress;
     – the key assumptions which might affect performance.
                                        (Audit Commission, 1984d, p. 38)

In their example the Commission shows for the planning officer as major tasks in 1984/5:

1.   Plan and implement moves to new offices.
2.   Improve response times on Development Control.
3.   Report on expansion of economic development and tourism potential (by December '84).
4.   Report of village initiatives.
                                        (Audit Commission, 1984d, p. 40)

As examples of Accountabilities the Commission includes:

*Accountabilities*
Development and Building Control Processes:
Ensure that all applications for permission under the Town and Country Planning and Building Regulations are processed in accordance with the law and Council policy, and that applicants are advised of the permissible development which best meets their requirements.

% importance.

*Goals*
i. Regain planning level of 85/90% in 8 weeks.
ii. Achieve 75% of applications for Building Regulations within 4 weeks.
iii. Ensure smooth introduction of scheme of delegation to officers.

*Performance Measures*
i. DOE quarterly statistics for 1st quarter '85.
ii. Internal quarterly report.
iii. Review operation end January '85.

*Assumptions*
i. No significant increase in workload. Additional staff resources made available. No new local plan or policy work undertaken.

(Audit Commission, 1984d, p. 41)

A number of local authorities have introduced systematic approaches to accountable management. In East Cambridgeshire a system of accountabilities has been introduced because it has been recognised that:

a) it is not sufficient just to preside over and process the existing conventions and structures of local government, but that these should be examined ...

b) To ensure that there is clarity as to where the real responsibility for results should lie (i.e. concentrating on outputs required, not professional inputs) through ...

c) The precise definition of jobs, and what they are there to achieve individually (as opposed to the discharge of functions through a collective of professions) ...

d) Emphasising the total accountability of line managers for the management of their services and the accountability of the professional support services for the effectiveness of the support they can offer them ...

e) The welding of the whole into a clearly planned, directed and renewable policy framework and operational machinery which provides elected members with the signals and levers that enable them to determine and control how they want East Cambridgeshire powers and duties to be exercised.

(East Cambridgeshire, 1984)

These principles have led the authority to develop accountable management. Accountable management involves not merely the formal framework, but managerial relationships. Managers set their key tasks and accountabilities with their superiors and in that same relationship account for what has or has not been achieved. Performance is assessed in relation to targets. Problems preventing effective performance can be examined and ways of overcoming them can be worked out. That is the bond of accountability which accountable management requires.

Accountabilities represent enduring and fundamental requirements of the job. If not achieved, the job holders are not successful in their jobs. Rigorously drafted accountabilities thus focus the attention of the job holder and his employer on what is expected from the job. This forces questions about relative priorities for the devotion of effort on particular parts of the job – according to what are currently critical aspects; on what should be the agreed and fair measures against which subsequent performance can be assessed: on specific goals to meet in the next 12 months; on the assumptions and constraints as to resources, and the collaboration of others which may affect the feasibility of reaching the level of overall performance, or specific goals aimed for.

(East Cambridgeshire, 1984)

It is argued that this process clarifies the nature of management responsibility, provides an opportunity for the managers to discuss problems in achieving their responsibilities. The process gives the managers clear guidance on how they will be held accountable. A basis is established for accountability. Often quantitative targets are established to remove, it is hoped, ambiguity from judgement on performance. The process provides the basis on which the manager's career, training and even, in some instances, rewards, can be considered.

The process makes explicit what is often left implicit by traditional management but which is required for effective control – what an officer is expected to achieve and the assumptions that underlie that expectation. Because what has to be achieved is made explicit, it is open to discussion and, where necessary, challenge. The process provides a pause, in which each officer and superior can reflect systematically on the officer and performance. It is a pause in which the focus is on the whole, and not on the specific incidents or specific tasks which necessarily make up normal contacts. The often repeated remark, 'I am assessing performance and giving guidance throughout the year – so no special procedures are required', ignores the difference between assessment of the specific of performance, and assessment of performance as a whole, in which strengths and weakness can be considered together and related to the organisation as well as to the individual. Counselling involves a pause for reflection.

Accountable management provides a basis both for the devolution of management responsibility and for accountability for that responsibility. There are, however, dangers for the new management if the approach is applied in too restrictive a way. More is involved in the work of the community manager than can be specified in the routines of this process. The community manager requires a responsiveness to community and to political purpose which cannot always be specified in advance.

The danger is that routines routinise. The resulting emphasis may be on the achievement of specified tasks rather than on innovation and learning. The achieved target may drive out the unachieved idea. Less priority may be given to the new ideas or to responsiveness to unanticipated problems.

Nor is the danger overcome by including in the specified targets a requirement that the manager 'should have three good ideas', 'show two examples of initiative', or 'respond positively on four occasions to community demands'. To suggest such performance measures is to show their absurdity.

Performance measures and targets or goals in relation to those measures are important. Bexley has established performance measures across the whole range of its work. The environment health department has response rates as targets for each category of request for service. There are target occupancy rates for each category of residential institution in social services. These are important to effective control, but performance measures cannot encompass all that is involved in a service. Nor can accountability be restricted to accountability for achievement of those measures. Devolution of management responsibility must provide organisational space to develop the role of the community manager. The new management require forms of accountable management that encourage responsiveness in action with the overall policies of the authority.

Much of this is conveyed by a report in Devon by a Working Party on Information, Management and Planning Strategy, as a result of which pilot projects are to be undertaken in building accountability centres. It argues that an accountability centre should be:

... a way of providing the best and most relevant services to the local community, as efficiently, effectively and economically as possible, based upon corporate, functional, and sectional plans ..., and with the ability to hold the local manager to account for the delivery of the services and consumption of resources under his control.

(Devon, 1985, p. 39)

This was, however, seen as a means of ensuring that the centre 'should be able to develop its own "culture" within which the staff operate' (Devon, 1985, p. 39). To this end it was argued that within overall plans and programmes the authority should:

Allow local managers (responsible officers) the maximum freedom within clearly defined policy guidelines to decide how to deliver the service they are responsible for, and hence the expanding of resources ...

Provide the means for local managers to understand the needs of their local communities better ... and through the delegated freedom to translate those needs into services, and thus be more responsive to the local community in the determination of priorities ...

Through this greater freedom and responsibility, to improve the motivation of managers and thus meet the aims of the concept by encouraging managers to develop a style to suit the community they serve.

Facilitate innovation, exchange of ideas and hence continually improve service provision.

(Devon, 1985, p. 40)

It is this emphasis on responsiveness in action that distinguishes the approach given by the new management from some forms of accountable management.

# THE COMMUNITY MANAGERS

The local authority officers act in the public arena. They are community managers, whether they are directly involved in and with the community, or indirectly working in offices away from direct contact with the public. The managers are subject to the pressure of demand and protest and face the politics of implementation. The politics of implementation involve the officers with councillors as well as with the public. Councillors act as advocates for their constituents and for their areas.

Over and above any formal relationship, the community managers seek wherever possible to develop contacts with councillors. A ward councillor or a member of the relevant committee can be drawn on by the community manager for advice. The community manager gains from these contacts. Councillor advice can form political sensitivity. Such contacts do not lessen the community managers' responsibilities. They are part of the network of pressures that they have to manage and from which they have to learn, and learning is at the heart of the devolution of management responsibility to community managers.

Devolution of management responsibility does not remove the manager from political or community pressures. The reverse is true. In the proposal by Devon, an emphasis is laid on the role of councillors:

A vital strand is the potential contribution to be made by *individual council members* in their role as local representatives and 'sounding boards' of local opinion and feedback.

(Devon, 1985, p. 23)

In East Sussex in support of the decentralisation to patch teams in social services:

Locally based member panels supplementing the formal channels of communication act as the sounding board for local elected members, and offer a regular opportunity for operational staff to identify the implications of the process of change across the whole range of practical support tasks the organisation carries out in the community.

(Young, 1982, p. 22)

Political direction does not eliminate the politics of implementation. Decisions made by a manager can have important and unexpected political consequences. The decision to let a local authority hall may be a routine decision but can be a subject of major political controversy when the letting is to an extremist organisation.

The community managers cannot and should not escape from politics since they work in a political institution. The institutional requirements are necessary conditions of management responsibility. The great error is to believe that management at officer level can be defined separately from the institution in which management is set. It is only if the devolution of management responsibility is informed by the values of local government that it can be regarded as an expression of the new management.

These values must, wherever possible, inform the definition of accountabilities. The managers must have their responsibilities defined in ways that encourage this conception of community management. That conception cannot be expressed in routinised measures alone, but statements like 'to encourage complaints', 'to review public access', 'to invite suggestions', 'to build active contact with local councillors', 'to increase political awareness', should be amongst the statements that appear in the statements of account-ability – even if they cannot be expressed in measurable standards of performance.

The values have an importance over and above the statement of accountability, and must inform the work of the community manager. Listening and learning is an important part of the task of the community manager. Innovating and experiment follows from listening and learning. The experiments of the community manager are not the grand experiments of the local authority policy maker, although what is administration, when seen from the higher reaches of the authority, becomes policy when seen in the reality of the community manager's task. One tier's administration becomes another tier's policy. A new way of arranging library books to meet users' needs is in its own way an expression of policy for those who use the library. An encouragement of innovation and experiment is an important part of the new management culture, within which devolution allows diversity, and from which learning can develop.

For the community manager, review of performance cannot and should not focus solely on the achievement of prescribed standards. Effective community managers learn about problems they do not expect to learn about. They listen and hear of issues they did not know about. They have made mistakes they certainly did not intend to make – and have learnt from them.

There must be room in the appraisal of performance for such questions as:

- What has taken you by surprise this year?
- What have you done that you did not expect to have done?
- What has changed? What have you changed? What has changed you?
- What separates clients from non-clients?
- What worries your clients most?
- What does the pattern of complaints show?
- How do you ration services?
- What are you most proud of?
- What have you learnt?
- What would you like to see changed that is outside your control?

- What are the politics of your task? Who gains and who loses from it?
- What are the councillors thinking about your work?
- What are the public thinking about your work?

These and like questions are for the community manager, as much a part of accountability as assessing performance against prescribed standards. They do not generate answers but may generate learning.

The new management requires community managers who express its values in responsiveness as well as in direction. Accountability is the more required, but its forms must allow many differing forms of accounts to be given, for it is the unexpected and the innovative that lead to learning. Accountable management in a local authority has to achieve the purposes of local government.

The development of accountable management is not easily achieved. It requires change in attitudes and practice not merely from those to whom managerial responsibility is devolved, but from those to whom they are responsible. Issues about such changes may involve the trade unions from whom support is required. Not merely are such important changes required from staff, but there are technical problems to be resolved to secure adequate financial and other information at cost centres. The experience of those authorities who are developing accountable management is that it requires time and commitment over time. That commitment has to be all the greater if accountable management is to achieve the purposes of local government in responsiveness, rather than forget those purposes in routine.

## CONCLUSION

In detailed control political purpose has been lost and responsiveness cannot develop. Control is required to ensure political purpose, but that requires effective control, concentrating on what needs to be controlled.

A devolution of management responsibility enables management to deploy resources to achieve political purpose. That devolution allows within those political purposes a responsiveness to the community and learning from that responsiveness.

Devolution of management responsibility must be backed by accountability. Accountability is necessary not merely to secure performance geared to organisational purpose, but as part of organisational learning.

The devolution of management responsibility can establish the concept of the community manager, but that requires new understanding.

- The hierarchy of control can stifle management by the weight of the tiers.
- To control all is to control nothing.
- Detailed financial control and detailed establishment control prevent effective resource management.
- The devolution of management responsibility weakens the hierarchy, but strengthens the institution.
- If organisational values are accepted, that is more effective than an armoury of control.
- There are limits – financial and political – to devolution. Purpose is defined in the limits.
- Responsibility carries accountability.
- Accountability cannot wholly be predetermined in community management.
- Responsibilities have to be met, but responsiveness has also to be realised.
- The community managers add to the organisation's requirements since they add to its understanding.
- The community managers make their own accounts, as well as the authority's accounts.
- Both the community manager and the authority have to listen.
- Accountable management is transformed by a local authority that knows its task is local government.

# 9

# Extending the Limits of Organisational Choice

## A NEW AGENDA

The organisational structure of local authorities met the needs of traditional management. That structure remains built on the same basic elements in very much their historic form: service committees, departments based on the bureaucratic principle and a dominant professional culture. The building blocks of the organisational structures of local authorities remain largely unchanged by past structural reorganisations.

The issues that dominated the period from 1966 to about 1980 were marked out by the Maud Report on Management of Local Government (Maud, 1967) and by the Bains Report on the New Local Authorities (Bains, 1972). Those reports led to a strengthening of the corporate capacity of local authorities. That apart, local authorities reacted to the reports by restructuring existing elements in their structure. Committees were redefined, but committees were still treated as the dominant setting for the political process. The number of departments was reduced, but the bureaucratic principle was strengthened rather than weakened in the larger departments. Professional dominance remained. Where the Maud Report questioned the role of committees, seeking to change them from executive into deliberative bodies, the recommendation was rejected by every local authority. Because it challenged the organisational assumption of the inevitability of the service comittee, the proposal lay beyond the perceived limits of organisational choice (Stewart, 1983).

The basic elements are not a necessary feature of local authorities. The organisational structure is fixed more by tradition than by statute. It is an organisational choice whether that structure is maintained – even if that choice is not made explicitly. Organisational assumptions, although powerful, can be challenged.

In a changing environment and under the pressure of the new politics, existing organisational assumptions are beginning to be challenged. The taken for granted elements in the organisational structure are being questioned, at least in their monopoly on organisational thinking. The new management cannot fully develop within the existing structure.

The agenda of organisational concern is, therefore, widening. Past issues have become less important and new issues centre on:

- the exclusion of the political
- the committee mode of working
- the bureaucratic principle
- the departmental mode of working
- the necessity of uniformity
- the functional principle
- the dominance of professionalism

The Maud Report and the Bains Report provided an agenda of proposals. The new agenda is of issues. These issues may lead to many proposals or to none. For organisational change is itself a matter of local choice.

## THE MYTH OF THE NON-POLITICAL

Changing and more assertive politics has meant that the place of politics in the organisational structure of the local authority is on the agenda of concern for the new management.

Change has been taking place. Recognition has been given to politics in the organisational structure of the authority. Where one party has a clear majority an official setting is provided – a one-party policy committee, a one-party sub-committee, a regularly convened chairs' meeting, political leadership as members of the management team – for discussion on key decisions between the political leadership and chief officers. The political groups (and even, in some authorities, the party beyond) are given recognition in that organisational structure. Alexander has shown that some chief officers attend political groups (Alexander, 1982). There have been authorities, such as Berkshire, where the political groups are constituted as committees of the council. Some of these developments may be restricted by the Local Government (Access to Information) Act (1985), since only the informal setting will have the protection of privacy considered necessary for open discussion prior to proposals being formulated.

Changing politics has given a new definition to the role of the chief executive in practice, if not written into formal terms of reference. The chief executive's role has focused organisational response to the political priorities and policies of the majority party (or in the absence of a majority party, to help overcome inter-party dilemmas). Close to the political leadership, unattached to particular services and existing patterns of provision, chief executives are well placed to establish and develop this role if they have both political awareness and political sensitivity.

In a few, but an increasing, number of authorities, there have been appointments of political research assistants. The appointment is normally attached to the position of leader or chair. The assistants have no power in their own right, but support the councillors in their roles.

Political assistants or advisers are additional appointments and are distinguished from political appointments to the position of chief executive, to chief officer, or to some other position in senior management. There are signs that political appointments are also increasing. A political appointment is the appointment of an officer because of membership of a political party or because of political views, rather than for, or as well as, management and professional abilities. Normally it will be said that appointments were made of 'officers sympathetic to the policies of the council'.

The perceived need for such appointments may derive from failure by traditional management to respond to political purpose. The political appointment is an expression of political frustration. The political appointment creates its own dilemmas, unless it is recognised as such so that contracts of employment, career structures, and the pattern of management can be adjusted.

The organisation for politics is an issue for the new management:

- How far should the local authority go in organising for the reality of political control?
- Does such organisation require political appointments and what are the consequences?
- Should local authorities move even closer to the cabinet model or is that itself alien, not merely to past traditions, but to the new politics?
- Can the responsibility of officers to the whole council with its implications for access of all councillors to advice and information be maintained in the changed politics?
- Can the requirements of party politics and the requirements of open government be reconciled?

## BEYOND THE COMMITTEE

The committee system is on the agenda of organisational concern for the new management. Political processes can no longer be contained within the committee system alone. Debate and discussion move away from committees to other settings. One trend is to move more decisions into the wider political group, to the party beyond and into consultation with local groups and trade unions.

Another trend is to provide new settings for the political process. The committee itself may develop settings which in form and procedures escape from the pressures of executive decision-making. The seminar to explore policy direction (as with the Devon policy debate described in Chapter 7), the committee meeting without an agenda, or the meeting with one item only, are all examples of setting the councillors (and the officers) free from the constraints of the agenda. Settings have been developed which do not have the formal nature of the committee. Their character is denoted by such phrases as 'panels' or 'working groups'. Councillors can break out of the limits of their formal role, for these are policy or problem exploration settings not decision-making settings.

In Merseyside County Council:

> The inadequacy of the existing six-weekly cycle of committee meetings for the sort of detailed discussion and argument which began to develop was another issue which immediately became evident. It led us to set up such a variety of formal and informal working parties and sub-committees as to provoke at least one member to protest on grounds of public expense. Membership was not based on political affiliation but on willingness to give the necessary time, an example which met with an impressive response from the staff involved. In this climate, the poker-faced caution which traditionally governs the relationship between councillors and officers gave place to a common enthusiasm for the job in hand with singularly rewarding results. The achievement of a code of practice governing the storage on computers of personal information provided striking proof of the value of the exchange of opinions on equal terms between officers and members.
>
> (Simey, 1985, p. 153)

Another development is to establish roles for councillors over and apart from the role as chair. Councillors can be nominated, as in Islington, exploring a particular problem area. Such a development involves more councillors in the work of the authority, using the neglected resource of the backbencher. Roles of representatives on outside bodies could be given organisational support in the local authority, emphasising its role as local government.

In Suffolk County Council a working group was set up to consider the implications of the county council's appointment of elected members to outside bodies. As a result of that review, provision was made for initial briefing and reporting arrangements to such representatives.

All these developments add to rather than challenge directly the committee system. They reduce the committee in its formal role, and in doing that recognise reality. Yet they make more necessary that formal role. The more informal settings become, the more important becomes a formal mechanism to relate discussion to decisions. An authoritative point of decision-making is required. Formality creates a need for informality and informality creates a need for formality.

The issue can be raised as to whether, if the committee system is merely a setting for the formal recording of decisions, that could not be achieved more simply. The committee system itself could be challenged. The very existence of a committee draws items to its agenda up the hierarchy of control. The committee system centralises in its formality.

The committee system is likely to be subject to increasing challenge, but in the end the committee will probably be retained. The committee has a role, even in its formality. The committee ensures access and relative openness, and its existence gives opposition and backbenchers rights. Formal will be balanced by informal, settings for executive decision by settings for policy discussion, and focus on service provision by focus on problems and opportunities. The issues have to be confronted:

- Is the committee system necessary and what are its consequences?
- Can a committee escape from formality or is formality an organisational necessity?
- Is there a choice between the ministerial model and the diffusion of power model?
- Should committees be based on departments?
- How can new settings be developed that escape from committee formality, and how, once developed, can they relate to the working of the authority?
- Must councillors be either chairs or backbenchers, and must the backbencher remain an under-utilised political resource?
- Should a committee tear up its agenda – at least once?

## THE NECESSITY OF BUREAUCRACY

The new management has a high capacity for innovation and responsiveness to environmental change. The new politics sees the bureaucratic principles as imposing on client, consumer or customer the organisation's definition of the problem rather than responding to the problem as seen and felt. The dilemma is that there is a necessity to bureaucracy for the large-scale provision of services. The issue is not whether the bureaucratic principles can be totally dispensed with, but whether they can be modified in practice.

While the bureaucracy is an organisational necessity, it can still be modified:

- *Breaking up bureaucratic scale.* One argument for political decentralisation is not that it removes bureaucracy, but it relates the scale of bureaucracy to the limits of the political capacity for control.
- *Modifying bureaucratic elements.* One possible strategy would be to enforce reduction in the number of tiers in the hierarchies, leading to wider spans of control and hence less detailed control.
- *Breaking the link between professionalism and bureaucracy.* At present bureaucratic and professional authority reinforce each other. The less the professional structure is identified with the bureaucratic structure, the more professionalism becomes a protection against bureaucracy rather than its reinforcement.
- *Building countervailing organisation.* The bureaucracy of routine is countered by the avoidance of routine by a think-tank. Organisational support given to responsiveness counters rigid rule adherence. Areal organisation counters functional organisation.
- *Removing the need for large scale bureaucracy.* There are alternatives to the direct provision of services. Privatisation is not the only alternative. Regulation can replace service provision. Consumer control can replace bureaucratic control.
- *Avoiding the over-specification of bureaucracy.* The political art is to separate where uniformity and rule are required from where variety and discretion are possible. The necessity of the bureaucratic principles need not be a necessity for every aspect of an authority's work.

None of these changes eliminate the bureaucratic principles of uniformity, hierarchy or functionalism. They do, however, modify the principles in application through countervailing tendencies built into the organisational structure. A new balance may be achieved by the new management, but in that balance many issues have to be faced.

- Are alternatives to bureaucracy possible for service provision or can it only be modified?
- Are the principles of bureaucracy necessarily interrelated?

- Can the limits of bureaucracy be specified?
- If decentralisation is an escape from bureaucracy, is it also an escape from government?
- How can the bureaucratic be combined with the non-bureaucratic?

## THE DEPARTMENT AND ITS HIERARCHY

Traditional management has been based on the departmental mode, characterised by:

- direct provision of the service
- a hierarchy of control
- a chief officer, normally responsible to the committee
- employment of staff by the authority subject to the conditions laid down by the authority

The departmental mode has a powerful hold on organisational thinking in local government. Until recently the departmental was the only mode of working envisaged in local authorities. Alternatives lay beyond the boundaries of organisational assumptions.

That mode has great strengths in the direct provision of services. It is the mode normally established by the operation of the bureaucratic principle. It is likely to remain the main mode of working in local authorities, although the devolution of management responsibility permits the wider span of control suggested above, reducing thereby the tiers in the hierarchies of control.

That mode can be modified in its working. In the finance directorate of Hammersmith and Fulham:

> There has been a very explicit drive to alter the Directorate from a 'top-down' to a 'bottom-up' department. This was a very ambitious aim and it was never expected that it would be achieved in a single year.
>
> Defining exactly what is a 'bottom-up' approach is not easy. It does not mean the absence of 'top-down' management. Local Government is a hierarchy and it is the task of top management to set a clear policy framework to enable less senior staff to know what contribution is expected from them. But within the constraints of a hierarchy top management *actively tries to encourage the flow of ideas* upwards and *decisions to be taken at all levels*, not just at the top. 'Bottom-up' also means staff and management setting out to take and communicate initiatives rather than simply wait for instructions.
>
> (Hammersmith and Fulham, 1985)

Although the department and its hierarchy remain the main mode of working, new roles and new problems are leading to new ways of working requiring new organisational forms. In a changing environment and with a new politics the local authority moves beyond the direct provision of services to influence and to indirect action. New modes of working may be required. For the new management, alternatives to the department are on the agenda of organisational concern, even though those alternatives may be added to rather than replace the department:

- the contracting organisation, in which the service is provided under contract;
- the company or association set up by the local authority, either separately or with another organisation;
- user control of local authority facilities;
- a task force or working unit set up to undertake a particular task;
- units concerned with equal opportunities or related issues organised on a non-hierarchical basis.

The new management is based on the department but is finding new modes of working as local authorities find new roles. The issues remain:

- Can local authorities, set as they are in the departmental mode, find organisational space for new modes of working?
- Can those modes of working be reconciled with political control and public accountability?
- Do the new modes have relevance in the direct provision of services?
- What modes have yet to be developed?
- Why not a staff co-operative?

## THE REQUIREMENT FOR UNIFORMITY

Local authorities require a degree of uniformity in the provision of service. Yet the new management seeks the responsiveness in action that comes from a capacity for diversity. The dilemma is resolved by creating an organisational space for diversity within the limits set by the approach to control discussed in Chapter 8. The devolution of management responsibility pushes back the constraints of uniformity. It modifies but does not remove the bureaucratic principle.

Decentralisation, over and above the devolution of management responsibility, has been seen as providing an alternative to bureaucracy. By devolution, not merely of management responsibility but also of political responsibility, to neighbourhood levels, the bureau-cratic necessity can, it is hoped, be avoided. The community can relate directly to local authority staff. Professional and other staff can be responsible to the local community and to individuals within it, who can define services in relation to their needs rather than to the requirements of the profession and the organisation.

There are, however, deep dilemmas in decentralisation. There is a potential clash between community and individual. There are issues as to how the community determines its will. But however it is determined, there can still be a tyranny in imposition. There is a potential clash between community and staff, expressed in trade union opposition. There is a potential clash between community control and political control of the authority. The local community may demand action which runs contrary to the political principles of the authority. It may reject the authority's equal opportunities or race relations policy. A balance is required between political control and responsiveness, and between uniformity and diversity.

These dilemmas arise because decentralisation is advocated as an alternative to bureaucracy. The dilemmas can be resolved by recog-nising that while there is a necessity to bureaucracy, countervailing tendencies can be built into the organisation. The issue is not whether decentralisation can replace bureaucracy but how it can modify bureaucracy.

The aim of the re-organisation in the Council's work in Islington is to make services more accessible and to increase the speed of service delivery once need has been identified. To achieve this the Council is advocating, in the first instance, a partial reversal of the bureaucratic tendency towads centralised decision-making. Obvi-ously major policy initiatives will continue to be the prerogative of councillors. An element of neighbourhood control, however, will permit local needs and wishes to influence the nature of Council services. In addition, the decentralisation proposals advocate an increase in the autonomy of those staff dealing directly with the public. Most of these staff will be housed in Neighbourhood Offices the independence of which is to be ensured by the staff's capacity to manage an element of their own budgets.

Decentralisation is also intended to reverse the bureaucratic tendency towards strictly delimited and specialised functions. It is not feasible for Islington to break with the established division of Council departments and occupations. Greater flexibility and better communications between specialisms, however, are major means by which the authority aims to improve service provision. This is to be done, firstly, by the creation of new 'generalised' positions which, it is considered, will serve to integrate the various branches of council services. Secondly, it is to be achieved by housing the different specialist workers under one roof in the Neighbourhood Office. Within each office, it is hoped, there will be full co-operation across specialisms and the formulation of a multi-skilled integrated team.

Decentralisation also intends to modify the third principle of bureaucratic administration. It represents a departure from the practice of standard provision. Across the Borough under decentralisation, it is recognised that the style and method of service delivery in each neighbourhood may well differ. The intention is to match services much more flexibly to local needs and wishes as these become apparent to staff in the Neighbour-hood Office and are expressed by the Neighbourhood Forum. Once again, however, this is meant to be only a partial departure from bureaucratic practice. The Borough will lay down strict minimum conditions for all services and in some cases this will also represent a new departure. Racist, sexist or other discrimina-tory policies, for instances, could not be pursued by Neighbour-hood representatives.

(Heery, 1984, pp. 46–47)

There is a political requirement for uniformity, as well as a search for diversity in responsiveness. Issues are raised which have to be faced.

- What are the political limits to diversity? What are the require-ments for uniformity?
- Is uniformity unnecessarily enforced? How does an authority break the habit? Can good administration be redefined in diversity?
- How is diversity legitimated? Can the community legitimate diversity? By what means? Within what limits?
- Are area committees of local councillors, as introduced in Bir-mingham, necessary to decentralisation? How do they relate to other forms of community representation?
- Yet how is political purpose reconciled with diversity?
- Knowing the limits before decentralisation is better than finding them in conflict.

## THE FUNCTIONAL DIVIDES

The functional principle is one basis for dividing up the work of the authority, but it is not the only basis. Thus, it is possible to divide up the work of the authority into departments based on geographical areas. Professional and other specialist staff would not in this model be concentrated in one department but be spread between areas and have a direct line responsibility to the area manager. The area directors would then be responsible to the chief executive. Kings Lynn and West Norfolk District Council created a structure based on this approach at reorganisation.

It would, in theory, if not necessarily in practice, be possible to base the structure of the authority on client groups: children, old people, etc. Each department would include staff from different relevant professions or specialisms, as appropriate.

Each method of dividing up the work of the local authority has benefits, but also creates costs. Each provides an emphasis on a particular perspective of the environment and on a particular way of approaching problems. That emphasis is given at the expense of other perspectives. A functional emphasis is at the expense of an areal emphasis. The strength of one perspective is also its weakness. The complex of a changing environment is necessarily being fragmented to match the capacity of the organisation. Inevitably certain problems will be neglected whatever the principle of division, although the nature of the problems will vary with the principle. There is a need for a perspective that looks at environments and at the organisation across the divisions – however these divisions are made – not to duplicate the work of the divisions, but to complement them by identifying what cannot be identified within the divisions.

That is the case for a corporate approach. The corporate approach developed before many of the tendencies described in this book, pre-dating or anticipating the new management. The functional principle was the one principle clearly challenged by the Bains Report. It was argued that a corporate perspective was required to challenge the dominant functional perspective. A local authority had to have a capacity to consider the problems it faced and to review policies on a corporate, as opposed to a functional, basis. Structural protection and support for that corporate perspective was to be provided at officer level by the role of chief executive, supported by the management team of chief officers, and at councillor level by the policy and resources committee. The result has been to establish powerful new organisational interests, potentially committed to a corporate as opposed to a functional perspective. Those interests are represented by the chief executive and chair of the policy and resources committee rather than by the management team. Although the management team was cast for a corporate role in the Bains Report, it is largely composed of chief officers representing departmental interests. Organisational interests are not changed merely by creating a new arena of discussion, and the management team has not, in most authorities, fulfilled the corporate role given to it in the Bains Report.

In effect what has happened is not that the functional perspective has been replaced, but that local authorities have the capacity to complement the functional perspective with a corporate perspective. It has been recognised that the local authority needs both a corporate capacity and a functional capacity – in itself a recognition of the role of local authorities as local government as well as service providers.

The corporate approach was seen as a challenge to the functional principle, and in one sense it was. It challenged that principle as the sole organising principle. Because of the dominance of that principle, the assertion of the need for a corporate approach came to be seen by its opponents and sometimes by its advocates as a denial of any place for the functional principle. Where organisational thinking is based on a single principle, any challenge to that principle is seen as total challenge and may even be presented as such. In practice what was sought, and what has been to some extent achieved, was a balance. A countervailing perspective to the functional perspective has been established in the organisational structure of local authorities.

The issue remains, however, on the organisational agenda because, although the basis for the corporate perspective has been established in the roles of chief executive and chair of policy and resources committee, those roles may not receive sufficient organisational support. That support cannot be given by functional chief officers who deny their role in giving it. Nor can that support be adequately given by corporate units, separated from the main management processes of the local authority.

The real issue for organisational structure is the organisation of the corporate centre to support the chief executive's role. The division of responsibility between treasurer, director of administration, planner, personnel officer, and property services, and their relationship to the chief executive, is on the agenda for the new management.

The traditional centre may be too strong functionally, but too weak corporately. The centre may be too strong functionally because it concentrates specialist expertise in its own functional departments. Concentration of financial, legal, committee and personnel expertise weakens the devolution of management responsibility and detracts from the corporate role. The chief executive does not necessarily gain support in the corporate role from these central departments if they are identified as separate departments.

In Cambridgeshire the central departments have been reorganised and a headquarters office has been created based on the roles of chief executive, director of finance and administration and director of planning and research.

It is likely that the new management will increasingly raise, as it has already raised in some authorities, such issues as:

- Whether the budget and the structure plan should be the direct departmental responsibility of the chief executive?
- Whether there should be an executive office under the chief executive combining the central corporate departments?
- Whether there is an over-concentration of financial and secretarial responsibility in the centre?
- Whether the treasurer's and secretary's or director of administration's department should be combined?

The concern of the new management cannot be restricted to the corporate centre. The functional principle determines the provision of and access to services. It brings the strength of expertise to bear on problems faced. Yet more than the particular functional expertise may be required both to perceive and to deal with problems. Not merely at the centre does the functional principle need to be balanced by countervailing tendencies.

The devolution of management responsibilities, the reduction, although not the elimination, of hierarchical control, the encouragement of diversity, all create a greater capacity for cross-departmental working if the will is there. The structure can create organisational protection for such working. The chief executive provides such protection at the centre of the local authority, but the chief executive is far away indeed from the field.

The basis for organisational protection has already been suggested in area committees and the neighbourhood office. For local government, itself gaining identity spatially, with councillors elected for particular electoral districts, the spatial principle provides a strong countervailing force to the functional principle.

The spatial dimension is not the only alternative dimension, on which a local authority could operate, and the new management requires the capacity to assemble skills from many functions for differing purposes. The inter-disciplinary working group is already well established in local government, drawing together functional expertise to resolve problems facing the authority. Such groups are valuable if assembled to bring new ideas to bear upon an issue. The danger is that they become a permanent talking group which meets weekly, fortnightly or monthly, to pursue discussion beyond the original purpose. More valuable is the short-lived task force, which works on an issue and then is dissolved.

The functional perspective is one appropriate perspective, but the environment should not be viewed through functional perspective alone. The issues have to be faced:

- How can the strength of the functional principle be maintained in the provision of services while countering its weaknesses?
- Can local authorities encompass a spatial as well as a functional perspective?
- Can neighbourhood offices and area committees be reconciled with the functional principle?
- Will the devolution of management responsibility be restricted in impact by the functional principle?

## A PROFESSIONAL CULTURE

The new management places the dominance of the professional principle on the organisational agenda in so far as it restricts the capacity of the local authority to respond to environmental change and to focus on local political choice. There is already a growing tendency for some senior posts in departments to be recruited from outside the dominant profession. There are increasing examples of chief officers who do not belong to the dominant profession in their department, although that is more likely to happen in departments such as social services or housing, where the professional status is more recently or not yet fully established. The new management may go further in challenge. There is perhaps little reason why a chief education officer should always be an ex-teacher, whose practical experience is, in any event, long outdated. Nor is it by any means clear that responsibility for the budget should rest with the accountant.

There is likely to be greater mixture of professionals and non-professionals in departments. That by itself would be a significant change. Departments with different professions among senior staff will also be significantly different from departments where the senior staff are all drawn from one profession. In a multi-disciplinary department organisational values have to be built; they cannot merely be assumed. What is built can be built for present management and not for past professional tradition.

These issues have already had to be faced where departments have been grouped in new ways bringing together different professions:

departments of finance and administration, departments of housing and environmental health, directorates of leisure services, departments of planning and transportation, directorates of technical services. In some shire districts such groupings have been taken further with the number of chief officers being reduced from the seven recommended by the Bains Committee for small district councils (chief executive, treasurer, director of administration, planner, housing manager, chief technical officer, and chief environmental health officer) to only two chief officers, as in Rossendale (borough director and director of operations), or to three as in East Cambridgeshire (chief executive, development manager and housing and environmental manager).

At the very least such changes remove the clear identification of the position of chief officer with a single profession. Such changes open the way to more radical new grouping of skills or the eventual erosion of traditional professional boundaries. At present the professional definition of tasks is written into organisational structures. The new management may need to write its own definitions.

The professional principle will be an influence on the structure. It need not, however, remain the sole determinant of organisational divisions. The new management is likely to move organisational management on from the grouping of departments to debate on whether and to what extent organisational structures should cross professional boundaries. Interesting questions can arise:

• How necessary is the dominance of professionalism to the management in local authorities and how far can it be changed?
• Can professionalism itself change, or can only its place in the structure be changed? Can a new professionalism be built on the values of local government?
• What are the consequences of the advance of the non-professional in senior management?
• Must the local authority view the environment through professional eyes? What other eyes are needed?
• Can structures be built that ignore professional boundaries?
• Can the professional principle be maintained for its strengths, but modified for its weaknesses?
• Can professionalism recognise the role of politics in local government as a strength?

## CONCLUSION – THE EXTENDED AGENDA

For the new management the debate has been transformed. The agenda of organisational change no longer focuses on a regrouping of elements in the structure. It is the elements that are questioned.

The outcome is likely to be not that any elements will be eliminated, but that they will be balanced by other elements. From questioning comes understanding and in that understanding the dominant tendencies supported by present structures can be identified. These tendencies are required for service provision but countervailing tendencies for local government need organisational support:

- rather than deny politics, it can be recognised in the structure;
- to the formality of the committee can be added the informality of new setting;
- although there is a necessity to bureaucracy, that does not exhaust organisational possibility;
- new tasks cannot all be constrained within departmental hierarchies, so new organisational forms arise;
- there is space for diversity within required uniformity;
- because a local authority has a functional capacity does not mean it cannot have a corporate or indeed an areal capacity – the world can be looked at in many ways;
- the local authority that does not accept the dominance of the professional culture can build its own.

New elements, if added to existing structures, can transform organisational dynamics because they express the organisational values denied by the present structure.

No firm proposals are put forward. The organisational debate has been transformed from sets of proposals as put forward by the Maud and Bains Reports, to organisational issues which can be resolved in different ways in different authorities. The new management seeks not the organisational uniformities of service provision, but the diversity of local government. Change in organisational structure involves local choice. Yet change in structure by itself is likely to prove ineffective unless supported by change in staff policies and processes. Structural change alone is not enough.

# 10

# Realising Staff Potential for the New Management

## FROM PASSIVE TO ACTIVE

At least until recently staff policies and processes have not been regarded as a major element in management. Traditional management focused on the continuities of service provision. Stability managed itself. There was little perceived need to build up a commitment amongst staff to the authority. Staff attitudes have often been regarded as beyond the concern of management. 'Low morale is inevitable in a period of cutback'; 'There is no longer the same motivation'. Such statements are an excuse for inaction rather than a stimulus to action.

In so far as the authorities (as opposed to personnel departments) have emphasised staff processes they have emphasised detailed control of staff numbers. In too many authorities, as posts randomly fall vacant, decisions on the filling of these posts have been taken by leading councillors remote from the operations carried out. It has been a classic example of substituting detailed control for effective control.

Traditional management relied for most of its senior officers and for all of its professional staff upon processes of socialisation that were beyond the control of the local authority. Organisational values were built up not by the local authority but by professionalism.

The influence of professionalism went deeper. The professional was assumed to derive his motivation from professional values, and in growing services that reflected those values. The professionals managed themselves. Motivation came from a sense of professional achievement in the growth of services. When growth turned to restraint, traditional management had no response for the problems of morale and motivation.

While passive staff policies met the conditions of traditional management, the new management requires active staff policies and processes to support those policies. It is concerned to build new organisational values, and to build a learning, adaptive and purposive organisation expressing those values. Neither of these can be achieved without positive staff policies and processes. Those policies and processes should secure that:

- processes of socialisation build an organisational culture for the local authority as local government;
- processes of staff development are established for the learning and adaptive organisation;
- staff policies and processes focus on staff motivation.

The new management ensures that all the various instruments of staff policy are geared to these needs. Training, career planning, selection systems, rewards, methods of payment, working conditions, trade union relations, communication and information can reinforce both the values and purposes of the new management. Their design and redesign are the centre of attention. Each is an instrument both for building, maintaining and changing organisational culture and for achieving organisational change.

## STAFF COMMUNICATION

The new management requires active departmental, authority and cross-departmental communication policies to ensure that staff generally are aware not merely of their own responsibilities but of the policies and purposes of the authority.

Organisational values are built, in part, by communication. The messages emphasised convey directly and indirectly signals to staff. Communication operates both ways, for the senior management of the local authority need the knowledge and the ideas of staff as much as they need to convey their own messages.

A communication policy has to be related to the circumstances of the local authority and of the department. The numbers of staff involved, their physical location and their working patterns vary greatly from authority to authority and department to department. Communication in a large shire county employing 30,000 staff involves very different issues from communication in a small shire district employing 450 staff. Communication in a treasurer's department in a metropolitan district, all of whom work in the town hall, is very different from communication in an education department, where staff work in schools, colleges, youth centres and across the city.

Although there can be no standard communications policy, there has to be a policy. If communication is merely allowed to happen, it is likely to happen, but not as intended by the authority. There will be communication, for messages are given to staff even where there are apparently none, and rumour can be built on single words or absence of words as well as upon many. What is not said communicates much.

Communication, to be effective, needs a redundancy of channels, above all for important messages. Over-dependence on single channels distorts both upward and downward communications. A chief officer who seeks to learn from the field-workers needs many channels, for each channel carries its own distortion. In the same way, to communicate to staff requires messages repeated in different ways and heard in different contexts.

Communication policy must involve management by walking about (Peters and Waterman, 1980). Chief officers must be seen and heard, and must listen to staff. Time is required if chief officers are to ensure that they are in touch with their staff and to ensure that staff appreciate the authority's or the department's policies. The messages given by visits should focus on a limited number of issues. Thus chief officers concerned to build up the public service orientation ensure their messages endlessly reinforce that concept. They emphasise learning from the public, ask how quickly complaints are dealt with, ask about the subjects complained about, and by their questions indicate importance. In these visits the chief officer listens to what is said and to what is happening about them. Listening can be shown in response.

The chair and leading councillors should be seen by staff to ensure their key policies are understood, but also to demonstrate by their visits a commitment to staff, and to provide an opportunity for staff to question and to challenge them.

Communication can take many forms and a communication strategy can and has involved many of these forms:

- interlocking work groups within the hierarchy as a means of learning and listening;
- regular monthly or periodical meetings of senior staff in all departments to discuss key topics facing the authorities;
- annual meetings for all staff, to learn about the budget and policy plan from the chief executive or chief officers. These meetings can be held on an area, a departmental or a divisional basis within a department, depending on size and geography;

- question times regularly held by leader, chair, chief officer or chief executive;
- small group meetings, on an *ad hoc* basis, of staff with a chief officer or chief executive;
- a journal or newsletter – in Warwickshire, *Beartalk* is partly written by the chief executive;
- a question procedure by which any staff can send in a question to be answered, the results being published monthly, called, in one American example, *The Right to Reply* (Barbour *et al.*, 1984);
- induction courses to build an understanding of the nature, purposes and culture of the local authority;
- training programmes as part of the processes of staff communication to build understanding of the nature of the authority's purposes and policies;
- staff seminars for councillors and officers (with the possibility of officers being drawn from different levels in the hierarchy) to discuss key problems and issues;
- an emphasis on the need for ideas and suggestions, with publicity given to, and comment on, those received;
- senior staff working for short periods with field-workers or in a school or residential home, and communicating in that action their commitment;
- opportunities for field staff to work in headquarters.

Rewards are communications. Staff too often feel themselves the unrecognised and unrewarded resource of the local authority. Too many a local authority speaks not of its successes, or if it does, ignores the contribution of the staff. The reverse can apply. Attacks on performance are part of the adversary nature of politics, which is one of the strengths of local government management, since it ensures a background of open criticism and questioning that is not part of the management of other organisations. The same style can easily carry over into direct and public attacks on staff. Such debate and diatribe can too easily be seen by staff as criticism of themselves rather than of the other party.

The adversary style can be carried over by councillors into staff relations. The staff are regarded as belonging to 'the other side'. Their performance and attitudes can be attacked. Yet it is only through and with the staff that the council can achieve its policies.

A local authority has to communicate to motivate its staff. Hampshire County Council have argued that:

There is a very large measure of agreement that the main influences on employee motivation are:
a)  Having a satisfying job.

b)   Knowing how this job fits into the overall scheme of things.
c)   Knowing what standards of work are expected (quantity and quality).
d)   Knowing that performance against these standards is being assessed and consequently knowing how well management consider the job is being performed.
e)   Knowing that good performance is rewarded and bad performance penalised – though rewards should not be considered in solely financial terms.
f)   Having some opportunity for career progression.
g)   Being rewarded by adequate and equitable salary and conditions of service.

If this analysis is correct, then there is a good deal that managers can do to enhance motivation as part of their normal mode of working. In particular, they can:

a)   Ensure that their staff are well informed about the purpose, plans, policies and objectives of the service or function they are working in: and of the broader County Council setting within which all the services operate.
b)   Ensure that individual staff (and each section or team) know what is required of them, the standards which are sought, and how well they are actually performing against these standards.

(Hampshire, 1985)

The local authority salary systems are probably too inflexible to enable payment to be the major factor in motivating staff. A local authority can use other means of motivating members of staff:

• the use of managerial devolution of responsibility to set challenges for staff and to appraise performance;
• opportunities for self-development and widening experience;
• recognition of good performance.

Each method – and others – is a means of communicating to individual staff. One could well describe many authorities as silent employers. It is so easily assumed that staff know their role, their priorities, their superior's views on their performance and the authority's policies. Silence communicates, but it does not communicate a positive message because all it communicates is lack of concern.

No active communication policy can be developed which ignores the trades unions. Such a policy should not threaten or replace the role of the trades unions in conciliation and in representing the interests of staff on wages and conditions of service. Nor should it threaten or replace the formal machinery of joint consultation. Indeed the growth of many channels of informal communication with staff makes the formal communication machinery important. Informality can too easily get lost. Formal machinery provides a fall-back position. At its best, the opening up of staff communication could lead to much richer and better informed use of the formal consultative machinery.

It has to be recognised that there will be circumstances in which there will be opposition between the trades unions and the local authority. There will be occasions, too, when the political decisions of the local authority are contrary to the concerns of the staff and the views of the union. There is, or can be, a clash between political control and employee interests, or between political democracy and industrial democracy. A clash cannot be avoided by avoiding communications. It is more likely to be aggravated.

A report for Lancashire Education Department by a working group on a sense of belonging (one of a series of four groups set up by the department in an imaginative initiative to examine the workings of the department) can be used to sum up this section:

> It was generally agreed that a greater sense of belonging amongst all staff could be better achieved not only by alterations to the *structure of management* but more importantly by examining closely *the style of management* that is operating throughout the authority.
>
> It was mainly a question of *how* managers managed, the processes they adopted, the caring that they demonstrated towards individuals, the genuine efforts that could be made through consultation to enhance the personal and professional development of staff and a better understanding of group dynamics with an ability to work more effectively in this context. (Lancashire, 1984)

## STAFF DEVELOPMENT

The development of staff is the other key process through which staff policies are established. A learning and adaptive organisation depends upon a learning and adaptive staff. It is through the development of its staff that an authority develops.

The first requirement must be the removal of obstacles to staff development built into past working of local authorities. Opportunities for growth by staff have to be widened.

The barriers to promotion and to widening experience need

critical appraisal. There are often many barriers in local authorities of unacknowledged discrimination. Some barriers discriminate at the recruitment stage. Others for training or for promotion. Discrimination against women is clearly evidenced by the low proportion in senior management, as is discrimination against the ethnic minority. The statistics are too clear.

There are other barriers that prevent the local authority using the full potential of its staff. The organisation of the local authority has internal barriers against development. The divide between manual and non-manual, the divide between professional and non-professional, the divides between departments and between tiers, restrict the development of the full potential of staff.

A staff development policy operates against these barriers, increasing movement across them, and providing staff with the experience and the training to make movement easier.

A learning and adaptive authority will require new skills and knowledge from all its staff and will challenge existing attitudes. This requires continuing staff development. Staff development can take many forms, apart from education and training, not least of which is work experience itself. Any process of staff development is likely to depend on support by provision for systematic counselling. Such provision must provide a pause for consideration by individuals and their superiors of performance and of development needs.

Such counselling and guidance can be introduced as part of a formal performance appraisal process, as in Cambridgeshire or Northamptonshire, but counselling and guidance can be developed without formal performance appraisal. In Lancashire job consultation interviews have been introduced on a voluntary basis in a number of departments:

> to provide the opportunity for some form of structured discussion or consultation between manager and subordinate covering such areas as
> a)    job identification and performance;
> b)    work problems and job improvement;
> c)    career prospects;
> d)    identifying mismatches of staff and jobs and examining remedial action; and identifying training and development needs.

The Scheme was seen as a two-way process, to the advantage of management in terms of improving work performance and encouraging more open relationships and to the benefit of staff from the creation of better, more constructive relationships with management, more job satisfaction and from assistance in furthering career development. The scheme was designed to supplement rather than substitute for, the regular day-to-day relationships and communication which should exist between management and staff. What the scheme did not purport to be was an instrument for assessing the suitability of staff for promotion or potential, discipline, salary grades or personal weakness.

(Lancashire, 1983, pp. 1–2)

The Joint Consultation Scheme provides for a prepared discussion between a member of staff and his supervisor. A joint note of guidance by the county council and the National and Local Government Officers Association branch to staff advises:

Joint consultation is designed to give you an opportunity to talk generally about your job with your supervisor. The purpose is to discuss any ways in which you can be helped to become more effective, possibly by furthering training or different responsibilities, perhaps by looking at particular problems which you may feel exist, possibly by re-thinking the way in which things are done.

You might think such a talk unnecessary because hopefully you are able to discuss things with your supervisor in the normal course of work. However, pressure at work and day to day problems often prevent really wide discussions developing. *The Job Consultation Scheme is simply a means for ensuring that each officer is able to discuss his/her job and any developments possible, at least once a year, but it will only be useful if both you and your supervisor prepare beforehand.*

Staff development can involve far more than normal work experience or education and training. Staff development can involve special projects, planned secondments, or indeed new moves in careers. Continuing development is for all staff and for all aspects of their work. It is, however, appropriate because of the nature of the book, to focus on developing officers for the new management.

New management requires officers with new skills, new attitudes and new experience. The officer of the past, and some of the officers of the present, define their role either in professional terms or in traditional management terms that exclude many of the concerns and much of the potential of present day local government.

The new management requires officers with:

- political understanding, sensitivity and awareness;
- a commitment to local government, and awareness of its special conditions and their rationale;

- an understanding of what goes beyond the profession in which they are trained;
- experience in and understanding of community groups;
- experience in and understanding of other organisations, both in the public and the private sectors;
- confidence to devolve managerial power;
- ability to listen;
- skill in policy analysis;
- a questioning, challenging approach;
- innovative ability;
- high tolerance of uncertainty and an acceptance of necessary risk;
- understanding of the management of influence;
- skills as a community facilitator;
- effectiveness in staff communication and counselling;
- a commitment to continuing learning and development;
- the art of organisational management (but of that, more in the next chapter).

The staff development policies of the local authority should build these skills, knowledge and attitudes. No officers will possess all these attributes. The new officers will not be paragons of all the virtues, but across the range of management these attributes will be required.

As suggested in a paper by the Finance Directorate of Hammersmith and Fulham:

> We are now recognising that management of the late 1980s in local government is likely to challenge the 'traditional' professional approach, which can be summarised (and perhaps caricatured) as follows:
>
> TRADITIONAL PROFESSIONAL
> *Rule orientated
> *Bureaucratic
> *Hierarchical
> *Generate paper
> *Risk averse
>
> What is needed is a 'new' professionalism, particularly in key central departments such as Finance.
>
> NEW PROFESSIONAL
> *Customer orientated
> *Problem solving
> *Good communications
> *Responsiveness
> *Sensitivity

(Hammersmith and Fulham, 1985)

# CAREER PATTERNS FOR THE NEW MANAGEMENT

Existing career patterns limit experience for many senior officers. New patterns can widen working experience for professional and non-professional. Staffing policies could encourage the development of careers that break down the rigidity of past patterns by:

- encouraging movement between central government, local authorities and other parts of the public sector;
- job exchanges with the private sector and the voluntary sector;
- experience as assistants to the political leadership;
- use of sabbaticals and special project work;
- the introduction to contracts;
- job movement – at least for limited periods – between departments.

The new management requires that senior staff have continuing understanding of the work of the field-worker and in public contact. At all stages of a career opportunities should be created for renewed experience in the field and in direct contact with the public.

New experience can be built into working careers. Working experience in an advice centre can be of value for officers whose jobs do not bring them into direct contact with the public. Work as a personal assistant to a chair, or work in a members' services unit, gives political insights and heightens political sensitivity. Most officers can gain from experience in a chief executive's department, while those who serve in that department, including the chief executive, would be better equipped for their work by experience in a service department. Without that experience, chief executives and their staff lack necessary understanding of service requirements.

The need for new career patterns does not end with appointment as chief officers as recognised by the report by the Institute of Local Government Studies and the Local Government Training Board on the development of chief officers, which identified three needs:

- to provide for the chief officer a breadth of experience and in that experience the opportunity for renewal and remotivation;
- to provide the chief officer with the opportunity to acquire new skills, new knowledge and new approaches to meet the problems and issues he faces;
- to provide the chief officer, and the future chief officer, with the opportunity to review his need for development and change and the skills to carry out that review.

(LGTB, 1982, p. 10)

It went on to argue that:

At present the normal career for a chief officer is to gain experience by movement between authorities and jobs until the position of chief officer is achieved. He may then remain in that position for a period of twenty or more years.

... because chief officer development is currently so firmly based on the way the career system operates, thought has to be given to that system. Also, because of changes which are occurring in staffing levels, there are issues about its continuing operation. We argue that local government should give serious consideration to:

i)      Long term aspects of career change.
ii)     New types of post.
iii)    Career guidance.

These are each put forward as providing the opportunity for a chief officer to gain new experience and in some cases new motivation.

*Career Change.*

A chief officer, once appointed has normally only two significant opportunities for career change. He can be promoted to a larger authority but often enough the financial incentives for such movement are seen as limited and there are obstacles in movement from a small authority to a larger authority as experience in a smaller authority may not be seen as relevant to experience in a larger authority. He can seek appointment as a chief executive, but this is difficult for other than Treasurers or Secretaries and Directors of Administration, nor is it clear that such an appointment would interest all chief officers.

In our view active consideration should be given by local government to how the opportunities for career change can be opened up. This could be achieved by any approach that:

i)      made it easier and more attractive for a chief officer to move from one authority to another;

ii)     made it possible for a chief officer in charge of one department in an authority to be considered for an appointment in another department of the authority;

iii)    made it easier and more attractive for chief officers of most departments to be considered for appointment as chief executives;

iv)     made it easier for chief officers in local authorities to move to senior positions in other public sector or private sector organisations.

(LGTB, 1982, pp. 10–12)

# TOWARDS A NEW MANAGEMENT CURRICULUM

The bias towards professional education can be corrected not by its elimination but by adding to it. Professionalism has a contribution to make to local government, but that contribution needs to be balanced by management development. However, the curriculum in management education for local government requires extension to meet the needs identified for the new management.

Management education normally covers such subjects as organisational behaviour, quantitative analysis and management accounting, personnel management and industrial relations. It can also cover the environment of the authority and its economic and social conditions and technological change, for management must be set in context.

There is a need to extend the management curriculum for local government so that it includes:

- political sensitivity, awareness and understanding – and management to achieve political purpose;
- the management of protest and pressure recognising their necessity in the public domain;
- the ethical dilemmas – not avoiding but facing;
- the management of rationing – understanding and guiding;
- public sector marketing – and demarketing;
- managing for public accountability – as positive purpose;
- building value understanding – exploring the values hidden in 'objective reports';
- budgeting processes for choice – not hiding the choice;
- community learning – beyond the services provided;
- balancing forces for change and forces for maintenance – the organisational dilemma.

The new management requires a new curriculum for management education, and beyond management education there is a need for specific training in the new skills required.

# CONCLUSION

The new management can only work with and through staff. A changing organisation needs change from staff. A learning organisation needs learning by staff. Staff policies and processes become for the new management an ever-present concern. This chapter has only covered some of the changes required. Within the broad range of such policies and processes, stress has been laid on communication both to and from staff, and staff development. Neither merely happens. Both must be worked at, and in the working challenge the reticence of traditional management. The new management cannot merely hope. The challenges are to:

- The chief officer, whose focus of attention is not on the staff but on the national scene.
- The chief officer who has no time to walk about because he is too busy 'doing his work'.
- The silent authority that does not speak to its staff.
- The political group that expects its policy to be adopted without explaining it.
- The chief officer who assumes that staff development can look after itself.
- The professional who believes development ends with professional training.
- The management course for local government whose curriculum treats politics as context rather than purpose.
- The management who blame 'it' on the staff.

Staff policies and processes for change must challenge.

# 11

# The Art of Organisational Management

## THE ORGANISATIONAL DILEMMA

Many changes have been suggested in the management processes, structures and staffing policies of local authorities. These changes are designed to support the new management for local government and its values. The issue might be thought to be the management of change, but the new management requires not a particular set of changes, but learning, adaptation and choice. The new management is not fixed but changes in the government of a changing society. The test is not the once for all management of change, but the continuing management of changing.

A local authority is, however, not only a political institution constituted for local government. It is a provider of services and that role must remain, for many of its staff, a dominant part of their work. The new management cannot replace management geared to service provision. The local authority may add to and even modify traditional management but it must meet the requirements of service provision. The problem is, therefore, not how local authorities can express their role as local government, but how they can combine that role with that of service provision, granted that each has its own requirements.

Over time the necessary absorption of service provision can limit the capacity for local government. The organisational dilemma is to resolve how an organisation can both maintain the stability for service provision and the capacity for changing. The dilemma has to be resolved not once, but in the continuing working of the organisation. That requires the art of organisational management grounded in organisational understanding.

## THE NEED FOR ORGANISATIONAL
## UNDERSTANDING

Management is carried out through organisations. Organisations in local authorities cannot merely be seen as neutral, transforming political will into effective action. The workings of an organisation condition the way problems are perceived and dealt with.

The organisation is the instrument that has to be used by management, even when organisational change is sought. Those responsible for management in local government – whether councillors or officers – work in and through and are conditioned by organisations. The new management of local government faces significant problems because change and changing is at the heart of its concerns.

To use organisation to effect change, to change organisation, or indeed to work in any way through organisation, requires organisational understanding. Failure to understand organisations can only frustrate management – for management has nothing else to work with but organisation.

There is an ever-present danger of discounting organisations. Because an organisation's influence is pervasive on those who work within it, its influence goes unnoticed. That which conditions thought can be hidden from those who are conditioned.

The local government officer can easily escape from the need for organisational understanding into the seduction of explanation by personality.

You can have the best organisation in the world, but it can be wrecked by personality problems.
It's not organisations that count in management but people.

Too often such phrases are not attempts to solve problems but excuses for evading them. To label a problem as a personality problem is seen as labelling it as insoluble, justifying inaction. A personality problem is defined as beyond the scope of action. Officers do not even have to consider their own responsibility for the 'personality' problem. They do not see it as *their* problem.

An emphasis on behavioural skills can be a corrective. Local government officers can learn to recognise themselves as part of the problem they had labelled as beyond their concern. They can acquire understanding of interpersonal relations and skill in handling them. Effective management requires sensitivity to group processes, skills in team-building and abilities to appraise, counsel and guide staff.

These skills have to be applied, however, in the special conditions of local government. Local authorities subject to public pressures and controlled by a political process face conflict as a condition of their working. Political parties divide in debate and in electoral conflict. They reflect divisions in society.

An over-emphasis on behavioural approaches can lead amongst the inexperienced to a belief that all problems can be removed and all divisions overcome through improved interpersonal relations. Problems cannot always be resolved merely by better group processes. Conflict and debate are the condition of government.

There is a danger, too, that an over-emphasis on organisational behaviour at the individual or group levels can distract attention away from a concern for organisation. It can encourage a belief that if interpersonal skills are well developed the organisational framework barely matters. Yet it is within that framework that group and individual behaviour develops.

Organisations matter because they influence behaviour. Those who have struggled in the history of society to change political institutions have been engaged in a purposeful endeavour. Those who have so struggled have known that institutions influence the ways decisions are made, and that the way decisions are made influences the decision. What is true of political struggle is true at other levels of organisational concern. The organisational framework enforces regularities of behaviour. Power to set an organisational framework is power not merely to influence the present but to influence the future. To determine that decisions will be made in a particular setting, to lay down a procedure specifying the way information will be arranged for the decision-maker, or to provide training in certain knowledge or skills for those who make or advise on decisions, is to reach out to influence the future.

The division of a local authority's work between departments or committees imposes a particular viewpoint of the nature of the activities of the authority, and how they are distinguished and linked together. To place the library service in an education department reflects and imposes a different view on the role of the library service from a decision to place it in a leisure and recreation department, or indeed in a separate department. The particular form of the budgetary process, the stages in which decisions are taken, and the information considered relevant, influence the outcome. A procedure that starts with consideration of the desired expenditure levels is likely to have a different outcome from a procedure that starts with consideration of the desired rate level. It is likely to lead the former to emphasise the needs that determine expenditure and the latter to emphasise limited rate increases. Processes of socialisation for senior staff in a department based on a particular proessional training are likely to mean that the problems on which the department concentrates most attention are those which that profession is trained to identify and to resolve, and that those problems will be resolved in accord with good profesional practice. Planning issues concerned with industrial development have too often been resolved by reference to planning criteria, which have at least until recently neglected issues of economic development and the need for employment.

Organisations matter, and the new management must, therefore, understand the instrument they work through. They must understand what tasks the organisation is structured to achieve with ease and what the organisation will find difficult to achieve. The new management does not rest content with the organisation they have inherited, moulded by and for the routines of service provision. The new management seeks change, but to change they have to work with the organisation they have. Organisations have to be used to effect change in organisations. But first they have to be understood.

## UNDERSTANDING ORGANISATION

Any organisation develops a way of life of its own. Behaviour that is accepted as normal in one organisation would be unacceptable in another. Command and uniform are the normal way of life of the fire service, but would be abhorrent to the education service.

There is a regularity to the working of the organisation. Within those regularities there will be many actions and many inactions – things done and things not done by individuals and by groups. There will be 'rebels' and 'conformists'. Indeed their very existence is part of the way of life of the organisation. They take place within an established way of life. The way of life of an organisation is a strength, enabling it to operate beyond the scope of the formal organisation. An organisation can be brought to a virtual halt by working to rule.

The way of life of the organisation is not, however, independent of the organisational framework, but is deeply influenced by it. The organisational framework, set by structure, procedures and processes of socialisation, defines the space within which the way of life develops.

Each part of the framework can vary in the degree of definition or prescription and in what is defined or prescribed. A local authority normally structures a councillor's committee role, but not the role in the ward or electoral district. Procedures can specify in detail the criteria to be applied, as when a housing allocation scheme prescribes the way points are awarded to determine an applicant's place on the housing waiting list, or allows discretion to a social worker for the exercise of professional judgement in handling cases. The degree of structuring and specification determines the space in which the way of life of the organisation develops, although space can be sometimes found even where none is prescribed. Discretion finds a way to act. 'Turning a blind eye', 'I'll only give you a warning this time', 'We'll enter it like this on the form', are ways in which inappropriate specification can be made to fit better an uncomfortable reality. Although space will be found, it will normally be a limited space within the organisational framework.

Those who prescribe the framework seek through that framework control over those who will work within it in order to achieve organisational purpose. The danger is that over-specification can limit organisational effectiveness in constraining unduly the organisation's way of life and its responsiveness to variation and to change. Those who prescribe have but limited knowledge of the events to which prescriptions must apply. The danger of over-specification has a counter-part in under-specification. An under-specified organisational framework can also limit organisational effectiveness by failing to clarify organisational purpose.

The organisational dilemma confronts the choice between limited specification to meet the need for learning, adaptiveness and responsiveness, and detailed specification to ensure the continuities of service provision.

## ORGANISATIONAL CULTURE

Organisational culture shapes the way of life of the organisation. The culture includes beliefs about the environment, assumptions about behaviour both inside and outside the organisation, values attached to the activities of the organisation, norms of behaviour and a language of organisational conversation. The culture is likely to have an internal coherence. Values condition beliefs and assumptions, and support the norms of behaviour. The words used – 'client', 'caring', 'pollution', 'development' – in departments express, and the interpreted by, those values, assumptions and beliefs. Culture powerfully influences the working of organisations.

Culture both reflects and is conditioned by the organisational framework. The culture is influenced by the structure and procedures of the organisation, because those can determine how the environment is perceived and the way activities are undertaken. Procedures can legitimate certain behaviour and form the language of the organisation.

The processes of socialisation are probably the most important part of the organisational framework in determining its culture. In socialisation beliefs grow, assumptions are made, and attitudes form. In local government the dominant processes of socialisation of professionalism and experience tend to make the department the focus of organisational culture. Professionalism and working experience are bounded by the department. In the department organisational history is made and told. Past disasters and past successes leave their mark in folk-tales. Former chief officers, perhaps not even in the present authority but in some past pre-reorganisation authority, can become departmental folk-heroes or folk-heroines. The bust of Henry Morris is still to be found in the office of the Cambridgeshire Director of Education.

Professionalism is the major force in forming departmental values, assumptions and beliefs, which is what professional training seeks to inculcate. Professionalism sets a language, enforces norms of behaviour and puts values on particular activities. The professionals look outward into the environment and see what they are trained to see and do what they are trained to do – whether it is social work, consumer protection or environmental health. Departmental history is professional history and the legendary figures – Morris, Clegg and Newsam in education departments – may not even have worked in that authority. Loyalty lies to the profession not to the authority.

Although the department is normally the main base for organisational culture, there are other bases. The work of local government encompasses semi-autonomous institutions, such as schools and colleges, with their own ways of life and histories, protected in their organisational culture by professional autonomy and past legends of headmaster authority. Even within the main department, there will be subcultures centring on less important professions or even the anti-culture of neglected groups. An amalgamated department, such as a directorate of technical services, composed of powerful professional groups – engineers, architects and planners – will not easily achieve a new departmental culture and may remain fragmented into the separate cultures of organisational history.

There can also be an authority culture. The traditional management of local government, concentrated as it has been on the provision of services, has encouraged the development of organisational cultures based on the departments that provide the services. Yet local authorities have never been able to avoid the conditions of local government. In their working they reflect something of the area they govern. There can be an authority-wide culture that extends across departments and that has its own history as well as its own heroes. The name of Joseph Chamberlain is still important to the pride of Birmingham.

## NOT AN EASY TASK

Organisational management is a major task for the new management if the organisational dilemma is to be resolved. Yet organisations are not easily managed. They have life of their own which is a strength and yet a danger if it restricts changing. The way of life of the organisation has normally to be worked with, for to work against it can lead to frustration. In working with the way of life of the organisation, it can be changed over time.

Organisational management is a continuing process. New directions have to be encouraged, not periodically but continuously. Values that the new management seek to establish must be continually reinforced. New initiatives need to be nurtured and protected.

Organisational management is not limited to a particular organisational change isolated in a moment of time. Certainly organisational management is not limited to structural change, for changes in structure made without regard to the way of life of the organisation, may often fail in their purpose. The culture of the organisation has to be managed. Local authorities which in the post-reorganisation era introduced corporate planning procedures and structures without regard for organisational cultures neglected socialisation processes. Those local authorities where forms of corporate planning were successfully developed recognised that it was a task for organisational management over the long term rather than a one-off organisational change.

Organisational design is a skilled task, although it is rarely recognised as such. There is a vanity in those who design organisation not as part of continuing organisational management but in the pride of their own certainties. It is as if one were designing a building without understanding the materials to be used. The organisational cultures that are fragmented and combined in structural reorganisations can distort and disturb the new organisation, not only at the outset but for many years to come. There is a special vanity in central government departments which in local government reorganisations design new structures for political institutions whose way of life they have never experienced, whose culture they do not understand, and who may themselves have but little or no experience in organisational design. For local government reorganisation to be undertaken in this way is as if a novice architect were given a cathedral to design as a first task, without understanding the materials used or the purposes to be achieved. Yet the vanity lies not merely in central government. In local government too organisational design is too often separated from the understandings of organisational management.

Organisational management requires the capacity to understand the organisation, to analyse organisational balances and imbalances, and appreciate organisational dynamics.

## ORGANISATIONAL LEARNING

Those responsible for organisational management must watch and listen to that part of the organisation which is their normal setting and by which they are themselves conditioned. They must watch and listen, so that they may reflect. Councillors may not be listened to by the senior officers. They are labelled and that makes listening unnecessary: 'not interested in policy', 'purely parochial', even 'pretty moronic'; so too can councillors label officers: 'against us', 'really a Socialist', 'really a Tory'. Watching and listening can turn on reflection to hearing.

It is necessary to watch and listen to the way of life of the organisation, to know its culture, not merely because it is what has to be managed, but because it conditions management. One can only manage a changing organisation if one appreciates what is taken for granted, not least by oneself.

At the top of the hierarchy it is hard to know of the learning at the bottom. Senior officers and councillors must watch and listen to those parts of the organisation for which they are responsible and with which they are least likely to be in touch in the normal working of the organisation.

Organisational learning requires reflection. Listening and watching are not enough. The patterning of the way of life must be appreciated. The values and assumptions that underlie organisational culture must be brought to the surface.

## UNDERSTANDING THE GRAIN

Organisational management needs to sense the grain of the organisation's working. It is easy to work with the grain, and hard to work against it. There are certain new activities that an organisation can encompass without hesitation; others over which it stumbles. There are certain directions in which the organisation moves naturally; others to which it has to be compelled.

A professionally based department will not readily undertake innovation which involves 'unprofessional' activities, although it will welcome an opportunity for 'professional' innovation and expansion. Social workers may resist political determination to emphasise the welfare rights component of their work at the expense of their 'professional' skills of social work.

A bureaucratic department will not easily break its own rules, although it will readily take on board a specific rule change. Thus if there is a political determination to make the department more responsive to individual problems, the tendency will be to express responsiveness in a new set of organisational rules going into even greater detail about how specific cases are to be dealt with, as special payments in social security led to new rules and regulations. An organisation will not easily work against its grain.

To detect the grain the manager may need to reflect on:

- What tasks does the organisation find easy?
- What tasks does the organisation find difficult?
- What is endlessly decided upon but never happens?
- What issues always raise disagreement and conflicts ending in frustration?
- What issues flow easily to solutions?
- What tasks are rarely mentioned as problems?
- What tasks are always discussed as problems?

In the patterning of the answers can be found the grain.


## APPRECIATING THE CULTURE

Organisational management needs to appreciate the values and the assumptions that lie within the organisational culture. Proposals that challenge organisational values, or that are contrary to organisational assumptions, are not easily established in the working of the organisation, although because values are rarely stated or assumptions made explicit, the source of the difficulties may be but little understood or appreciated. If it is appreciated, direct challenge to the values or to the assumptions may prove unnecessary. Other approaches might be found.

Organisational culture must be understood in a changed and changing organisation, if the organisation's capacity for self-managing is to be used purposively. Those who work across different organisational cultures face special difficulties, for they must understand not one but many cultures.

In the post-reorganisation period many attempts to develop the corporate approach challenged departmental cultures without an understanding of what was challenged. With understanding, departmental cultures might have been developed rather than challenged. Thus while the corporate approach was seen by many as an attack on the education service, that might not have been the case if the values of that service had been appreciated. The value placed by the education service on the development of the individual could have been sustained in the corporate working of the authority.

There will be a need for the new management to challenge departmental culture, but even then understanding is required. First, however, it has to be determined whether challenge is necessary. To demand output measures from the education service without regard to that service's past experience of the danger of overreliance on simplistic measures inevitably met resistance. There was a simpler way. Educational values could have been worked with rather than against. Educational processes are assessed continuously. Few professionals would deny that they can judge whether a school is working well or that they can tell a good teacher from a weak one. Such an assessment is based on many indicators. Far more would be learnt about judging performance from exploring the insights that underlie those assessments than would be achieved by the routines of output measurement.

Even within departments there is a need to work across cultures or subcultures which can be remote both organisationally and geographically from senior management. The cultural division between administrative staff who have often worked for their whole career in one authority, and the professional staff mobile in their careers between authorities, can be a barrier to effective working.

Particular working units have their own culture formed in response to their task. The awards branch in an education department has its own seasons and its own pressures. The world of meat inspection in environmental health, isolated in the conveyor belt process of an abattoir, builds a protective set of beliefs in that isolation. The world of home-helps in social services builds its values around practical help and in those values may resent the world of social work, perceived as theoretical and remote.

As with departmental cultures, so with the subcultures. Without understanding, subcultures can be challenged unnecessarily where they could have been worked with, for in those subcultures there are strengths to be used.

To trace the culture may be to learn the nightmare events that trouble a profession. Some treasurers said theirs was the destruction of all financial records. Or it may be to know what building an architects' department is most proud of and why. Or it may be to understand the language of 'sharing' in social work. From such understanding values can be found and a culture traced.

To appreciate the culture the manager may need to reflect on such questions as:

- What are the nightmare events that would destroy achievement?
- What are the successes that are dreamed of or told in the tales of the organisation?
- What special words are used in the organisation, and where can their meanings be found?
- What tasks would those in the organisation welcome, and what would they reject?
- What assumptions are held about behaviour in the organisation and outside?

In the answers organisational values and organisational assumptions may be revealed.

## KNOWING THE FOLKWAYS

Each organisation has its customs and habits, in part formed by the work. 'There is a pattern to a Treasurer's year. There is a yearly crisis and the rest of the year follows the seasons.' A treasurer moved from traditional folkways to the role of chief executive found no seasons. 'Instead, the job was the crises.'

In organisation there are folkways for action. Information runs along well established channels. There are points at which access is easier, and points where it is impossible. The experienced councillor knows the points for action. The new councillor has to learn through frustration. There are points in organisational time and space when action can be taken quickly. A crisis can be used to cut corners by those who know the way.

Those who work with organisation must know the folkways. One director of social services said:

The key to speedy communication to the field is to know the grapevines. You then know who to speak to to secure the messages are widely heard.

Perhaps the questions to be reflected on include:

- Are there seasons or rhythms to working patterns?
- What is the gossip?

- Where does one go for organisational knowledge and where for organisational wisdom?

## AND IN REFLECTION

An organisation has to be listened to. Patience is a technique in organisational learning. Learning requires more than watching and listening; it requires reflection. The regularities of the life of the organisations within the organisational framework are not visible on the surface. What is visible is organisational messiness. Patterning emerges on reflection. Reflection can be helped:

- Into any organisational structure lines of hostility can be easily built.
- There are points of leverage in organisation. If one can find the right point, one can move organisational mountains.
- Around blockages to actions can be found challenged assumptions, fractured folkways and cultural shock.
- Reaction builds counter-reaction, if one can wait.

The lesson of reflection must be that while the grain, the culture and the folkways are powerful in the organisational life, that organisational life can be influenced by the art of organisational management – its absence or its presence.

## THE ART

Organisational management is a continuous and continuing process. While not ruling out the possibility of radical organisational restructuring, that is not its main focus. Nor is the continuing process of organisational management made any the less necessary where such radical restructuring takes place. A focus on changing organisational structures has too often been treated as a substitute for organisational management. Given organisational management, a restructuring may be unnecessary. Given restructuring, organisational management is the more necessary if the structural change is to be effective in the working of the local authority. Not to appreciate this point is the structural fallacy.

The structural fallacy is the belief that management problems are resolved by structural change alone. Following the Maud Committee on management, many local authorities reviewed their organisational structures and set up policy committees to provide overall policy direction in the working of the authority. That may or may not have been necessary. The fallacy is to believe that the change itself resolves problems. Recently an increasing number of authorities have seen the need for a co-ordinated approach to property management, and as a result have set up property departments, amalgamating existing architects and estates departments. Again the fallacy is the belief that the change resolves the problem. In each case the problem might have been resolved without structural change, and in each case structural change alone does not resolve the problem.

Organisational management does not lightly undertake large-scale organisational restructuring. Such restructuring can often only be achieved through conflict. Restructuring directly challenges established organisational interests. Defensive and offensive organisational wars are generated. That may be necessary, but it is an organisational cost to be undertaken only if other approaches have to be ruled out.

The need is to consider how the problem should be overcome, and not to regard structural change as in itself a solution. Organisational management adopts a holistic approach to the working of the organisation. It focuses on all aspects of the organisational framework – procedures, structures and processes of socialisation – not in isolation but in their interrelationship. It focuses too on the way of life of the organisation, on the culture that supports it, and on the relationship between the framework and culture. Organisational management is based upon organisational understanding.

Organisational management recognises that most organisations derive their strength from their quality of self-management. Effective organisational management uses that organisational capacity for self-management, giving it a new direction rather than challenging it. Organisational management should normally work with the grain, modifying, but not cutting across, the way of working. Organisational values should be cherished wherever possible seeking their development rather than their denial.

With organisational understanding, it may be possible to achieve maximum impact with minimum effort. Organisational mountains can be moved if one works with the strength of the organisation. Actions that are most effective will use the flow of the organisation, although they modify its direction. The flow can be directed using its own strength, not by forceful change of direction but by gradual change. The changes carried out in authorities such as Cambridgeshire have been evolved over ten years.

There is a need to choose the right touch, at the right point in organisational space and time. At a time of public attacks on local government local authorities have found that an emphasis on the value of service for the public meets the needs for motivation amongst their staff. The conditions mean that the service message can be heard.

There are moments when organisations are ready for a particular change, and that change can easily be achieved. Change conditions can be cultivated. Changes grow and their roots are not easily to be found, yet their seeds can be sown. One person added to a working group can transform its working. A pause in routine provides organisational space for reconsideration. A small organisational change can change organisational dynamics and open up possibilities that lay beyond previous boundaries of organisational concern. To recognise an areal perspective by area committees gives a legitimacy to the 'parochial viewpoint' of councillors which can lead on to change, even when the area committee has no direct powers but only the scope to influence. Organisational management knows the potential of a stimulus and the danger of a blueprint. A stimulus can use the organisational capacity for self-management, while a blueprint can destroy it. Action is taken, but not over-specification. An organisation can change itself if the stimulus is rightly judged.

The argument of this section is not against organisational change. This book has argued the need for change and for changing. The argument of this section is about how the required organisational change should be effected, not merely at a particular point in time, but over time. The argument is that where change can be achieved with minimum disturbance, it will be most effective. There will be times when that is not possible. Such occasions need to be carefully prepared for and require maximum management attention. It is because there will be such occasions that care is required not to disturb other aspects of the organisation, when such disturbance could be rendered unnecessary by gradual approaches.

If change has to be against the organisational grain, then that has to be accepted. All the more reason for working with the grain where that can be done. The local authority has to meet the requirements of change for local government, while meeting the requirements of continuity for service provision.

## CORRECTING ORGANISATIONAL BALANCE

The critique by the new management is of organisational balance. The critique is not that an emphasis is placed on service provision, but that there is an emphasis at the expense of local government. The organisation of local authorities is dominated by the requirements of service privision, without being balanced by the requirements of local government. Organisational management should be directed at correcting the balance.

This requires a greater emphasis on:

- decentralisation as opposed to centralisation
- variety as opposed to standardisation
- change as opposed to stability
- openness as opposed to closure
- long term as opposed to short term
- corporate as opposed to departmental
- flexibility as opposed to rigidity
- diversity as opposed to uniformity
- political as opposed to professional

Not to replace the latter characteristics, but to provide greater organisational space for the former. From the perspective of the new management there is a present imbalance in the working of local authorities. Organisational management requires a reading of organisational imbalance to identify where emphasis is required.

There are no absolute principles of organisation. Thus there are arguments for centralisation in organisation, and there are arguments against. The arguments will gain or will lose strength with organisational circumstances. Yet in the end effective organisation is likely to involve neither the absolute of centralisation or the absolute of decentralisation, but an appropriate balance between them. Any organisational principle carried to excess is dangerous. A totally centralised authority would have destroyed initiative and responsiveness. But a totally decentralised local authority would lose its organisational identity and be incapable of giving expression to collective political purpose. A balance between centralisation and decentralisation is necessary for the effective working of a local authority. While certain decisions have to be centralised, others can be decentralised. The choice lies in the appropriate balance of centralisation or decentralisation in the circumstances of the organisation.

For the large-scale delivery of services and for council-wide political control standardisation may be important, but over-standardisation limits responsiveness. In variation can lie a matching of need and local political involvement, but too great a variation can destroy political purpose.

The organisation of service provision has its own need for stability. The organisation of home-helps or of street cleansing is designed to provide a certain and a reliable service. Local government, however, involves a capacity for change, both to identify the need for change and to implement it. Change may be required in the nature of both the home-help service or of street cleansing, but continuity of service provision has to be maintained through the changing.

Any organisation has to guard its boundaries to carry out its task. Organisational time and space has to be protected. A reception desk is necessary to prevent interruptions. A classroom door has at least occasionally to be closed to the outside world. Yet no organisation can be completely closed.

Many of the issues faced by a local authority have their own urgency; they have to be dealt with. Yet if the focus is on the short term alone, choice is limited. Some possibilities can be realised only in the longer term. Some problems only emerge over the longer term.

The departments are a focus of organisation for local authorities in their provision of services. The departmental structure is largely defined by the services provided. The local authority as local government has, however, to find another focus of concern if it is not to be limited in its working to the existing problems of services.

These and the other organisational dimensions illustrate the organisational dilemma. The organisational balance will not be resolved by determining which organisational principle to pursue, but the appropriate balance to be maintained between apparently conflicting principles. The issue is not whether the organisation should be based on departmental or on corporate working, but how an organisation can combine different patterns of working, and what the balance should be between them. The issue is not whether a local authority should focus on the short term or the long term, but how it can do both.

The issue of balance involves choice, and continuing choice. The problem of organisational management is not of a once-for-all choice, encapsulated in a new organisational structure. That is relatively easy to carry out, although uncertain of achievement. The problem of organisational management is to judge the balance not at a particular time but over time. A local authority can easily move from balance to imbalance. In a changing environment, the point of balance can change.

In any organisation one principle is likely to be emphasised more than its opposite. The countervailing principle may well require organisational protection. In a largely centralised organisation, attempts to decentralise will be eroded over time, unless actively protected by organisational management. In a largely service-based organisation, attempts to develop corporate working will be eroded over time unless actively protected by organisational management.

There is an ever present danger of organisational drift towards the dominant organisational characteristic.

The new management seeks a new organisational balance to sustain the local authority's role as local government. That balance will require protection against organisational drift, caused by the dominance of service provision in the work of the local authority.

## COUNTERVAILING FORCES

Organisational management corrects imbalance by creating countervailing forces in the working of the organisation. That has been the main argument of the book. Existing organisational elements are not removed, but are corrected for.

Organisational constraints are relaxed rather than removed to provide organisational space for change. A pause for learning is provided (Chapter 5). While organisational control is maintained, there is scope for responsiveness in management (Chapter 8).

New elements are added to the organisation to provide countervailing forces. New modes of thought are added by policy analysis (Chapter 6). Procedures to highlight choice in direction are incorporated in the organisational framework (Chapter 7). Where required new elements can be added into the organisational structure (Chapter 9). New processes of socialisation geared to the needs of the local authority for local government are added to professional processes (Chapter 10).

Procedures designed to create an organisational pause in routinisation must be protected against becoming a new routinisation – they must be themselves subject to review. Countervailing forces require organisational protection. As important, therefore, as new elements is managerial focus. If new elements in the organisational structure are to be maintained over time, they must receive managerial attention. Managerial behaviour in the allocation of time provides signals to the organisation.

## BUILDING ORGANISATIONAL CULTURE

More is required than focus. If the new management can develop an organisational culture that supports the values set out in Chapter 4, then changes in structure and procedures cease to have the same importance, and those changes that are required will be more readily accepted.

Managers give signals by their actions and their words. A chief officer immersed in professional issues signals to his staff that he stresses and expects to see stressed only professional values. A chief officer who clearly obtains, and is seen to obtain, his main satisfaction from involvement in national work for the local authority associations and for central government is signalling to his staff his lack of concern for authority issues. A chief officer who emphasises to his staff the constraint under which the local authority or the department operates signals a resistance to innovation. A chief officer who generates ideas and responds to staff ideas signals his interest in innovation. Unconsciously as well as consciously the chief officers build values into the culture of the department.

Words and questions reinforce values for they show the focus of concern. Stories will be told, myths will be built by incidents. One chief education officer trying to convey the message of self-help said to parents in a school that if they would agree to set aside a week-end to help decorate the school, he 'would come and paint the door'. They did and he did and the message went round the county.

Letters, memoranda, talks, reinforce values. For to build a culture, communication is necessary – not in one way but in many ways. Staff development and staff communication become a positive tool for building an authority culture. An authority culture requires as much emphasis in staff training and development as a professional culture receives emphasis in professional training and development.

Management that seeks to give a thousand different messages to its staff will find that none is heard. Management that seeks to concentrate on a limited range of values will be heard – provided the messages are repeated. Management moulds the culture in repetition, and the culture builds a new organisational balance. The starting point for organisational management will rarely be organisational structures but staff policies and processes that can build organisational culture. They lie at the heart of organisational management. New management must learn to build a culture that supports the values of local government as well as those of service provision.

## CONCLUSION

The search for a new management touches many different aspects of management. Without the art of organisational management that search will end in frustration. The new management seeks change with and through organisation. Organisation must be the instrument to change organisation.

- Organisational understanding is necessary for management of change and changing.
- Only those who can listen and watch, as well as talk and act, can understand the organisation.
- The capacity for self-management is a strength to be used.
- The strength of an organisation can be used to aid change or to frustrate change. Without understanding frustration is inevitable.
- To know an organisation one must know its folkways.
- Present organisational values are foolishly denied and wisely developed, but first they have to be understood.
- One can never be sure of organisational balance, but one can sense imbalance.
- The new management corrects imbalance by an emphasis on government, not through a once-for-all change but in continuing attention to organisational management.
- Organisational management uses not one instrument, but many, and effective management lies in their interaction.
- Yet to build and sustain an organisational culture for the new management is the foundation of success.
- The issue is what values underlie that culture. Commitment to values will signal its own message.
- The values must be those of the local authority as local government, for they set the purposes for the new management – and the search is how to achieve those purposes.

# Postscript

The government of a changing society requires to realise the potential of local government. A centralised system of government reduces the capacity of government in the uncertainties of a turbulent environment. If there was:

- a certainty of problem and response
- a stable environment
- uniformity of needs and wants

then a centralised system of government could cope, even if it could not involve. Such is not our present society, or any society that is likely to be. The government of uncertainty, change and difference requires the diffusion of power, diversity of response, closeness to community, and the capacity for local choice that can be provided by local government, if local authorities could realise it.

That realisation may be as much restricted by traditional management of local authorities as by central control. A search for a new management is required to realise the capacity of local authorities for local government.

That search has begun.

# References

Alexander, Alan (1982), *Local Government in Britain Since Reorganisation* (London: Allen and Unwin).

Association of Liberal Councillors (1985), *Local, Open and Efficient.*

Audit Commission (1984a), *Report and Accounts* Year ended 31st March, 1984.

Audit Commission (1984b), *The Impact on Local Authorities' Economy, Efficiency and Effectiveness of the Block Grant Distribution System.*

Audit Commission (1984c), *Improving Economy, Efficiency and Effectiveness in Local Government in England and Wales.* Audit Commission Handbook, Volume II.

Audit Commission (1984d), *Value for Money at Wansdyke.*

Audit Commission (1984e), *Improving Vehicle Fleet Management in Local Government.*

Bains, M. A. Chairman, Working Group on Local Authority Management Structures (1972), *The New Local Authorities: Management and Structure* (London: HMSO).

Banfield, Andy (1985), 'The unification of environmental health and trading standards', *Local Government Policy Making* (March, 1985).

Barbour, George P. Jr, Fletcher, Thomas W., and Sipel, George A. (1984), *Excellence in Local Government Management.* (Washington: International City Management Association).

Blunkett, David (1981), 'Towards a socialist social policy', *Local Government Policy Making* (Summer, 1981).

Bradford, City of (1984), *The Changing Face of Bradford* (District Trends).

Brooke, Rodney (1983), 'Crime prevention and local government', *Local Government Policy Making* (July, 1983).

Buchanan, C. D. (1963), *Traffic in Towns* (London: HMSO).

Bulpitt, J. G. (1967), *Party Politics in English Local Government* (London: Longman).

Cambridgeshire County Council (1984), *Medium Term Plan, 1985–88.*

Cambridgeshire County Council (1985a), *Corporate Ten Year Strategy,* a discussion paper.

Cambridgeshire County Council (1985b), *Medium Term Guidelines 1986–91.*

Devon County Council (1985), *Information, Management and Planning Strategy,* final report.

Donnison, David (1983), *Urban Policies* (London: Fabian Society).

Downey, Patricia, Mathews, Alison and Mason, Serena (1982), *Management Co-operatives: Tenant Responsibility in Practice (London: HMSO).*

Downs, Anthony (1976), *Urban Problems and Prospects* (Chicago: Rand McNally).

Dryzek, John S. (1983), 'Don't toss coins in the garbage can', *Journal of Public Policy* (October, 1983).

Fenn, Eddie (1983), 'Launching a local authority into the tourism market', *Local Government Policy Making* (Spring, 1983).

Fisher, Fred (1983), 'The new entrepreneurs', in Barbara H. Moore, *The Entrepreneur in Local Government* (Washington: International City Management Association)

Flynn, Norman, and Walsh, Kieron (1982), *Managing Direct Labour Organisations* (Birmingham: Institute of Local Government Studies).

Gibson, Tony (1984), *Counterweight: The Neighbourhood Option* (London: Town and Country Planning Association).

Glennerster, Howard (1983), 'Client group budgeting, a prerequisite for efficient care', *Public Money* (December 1983).

Goodrich, James A. (1983), 'Marketing for public managers', in Barbara H. Moore, *The Entrepreneur in Local Government* (Washington: International City Management Association).

Goss, Sue (1984), 'Women's initiatives in local government', in Martin Boddy and Colin Fudge, *Local Socialism* (London: Macmillan).

Grayson, Leslie (1978), *Library and Information Services for Local Government in Great Britain* (London: Library Association).

Hall, A. S. (1975), *The Point of Entry: A Study of Client Reception in the Social Services* (London: Allen & Unwin).

Hammersmith and Fulham London Borough (1985), *Management 1985–6* (Finance directorate).

Hampshire County Council (1985), *Employee Motivation* (Report by the Chief Executive to the Personnel Sub-committee).

Hardy, T. T. G. (1984), *Accountabilities – Management Development in the East Cambridgeshire District Council* (Paper prepared for LGTB seminar).

Heery, Edmund (1984), 'Decentralisation in Islington', in Robin Hambleton and Paul Haggett, *The Politics of Decentralisation: Theory and Practice of a Radical Local Government Initiative*. (Bristol: School of Advanced Urban Studies).

Heiser, Brian (1985), 'Qualitative research with users', *Local Government Policy Making* (March, 1985).

Hill, Michael J. (1972), *The Sociology of Public Administration* (London: Weidenfeld & Nicolson).

Hinds, Tom (1984), 'Local financial management: a pilot scheme', *Educational Management and Administration*, (Spring, 1984).

Hirschman, Albert O. (1970), *Exit, Voice and Loyalty* (Cambridge, Mass.: Harvard University Press).

HMSO (1983), *Financial Management in Government Departments*, Cmnd 9058, (London).

Holtham, Clive (1981), 'Flexibility in control systems and accountable management', *Local Government Studies* (March/April, 1981).

Holtham, Clive, and Palk, Nigel (1981), 'The need for more flexibility in financial management', *Public Finance and Accountancy* (March, 1981).

Humphrey, Colin, and Thomas, Hywel (1983), 'Making efficient use of scarce resources', *Education* (19 May 1985).

Islington, London Borough (1971), *Programme Structure*.

Jefferies, Roger (1982), *Tackling the Town Hall* (London: Routledge & Kegan Paul).

Jones, George, and Stewart, John (1983), *The Case for Local Government* (London: Allen & Unwin).

Kolderie, Ted (1983), 'Rethinking public service delivery' in Barbara H. Moore, *The Entrepreneur in Local Government* (Washington: International City Management Association).

Lancashire County Council (1983), *Job Consultation Pilot Scheme* (Chief Executive/Clerk's Department, Report of the Design Group).

Lancashire County Council (1984), *A Sense of Belonging* (The Report of a Management Development Group, Lancashire Education Department).

Leach, Steve, and Stewart, John (1984), 'Strategy and the case for metropolitan government', *Built Environment*, vol. 10, no. 2.

Leicester, City of (1982), *A Race Relations Policy – The Next Steps – Service Provision* (Report of the Chief Executive 9 November, 1982).

Local Government Training Board (1982), *The Development of Chief Officers* (Report prepared with the Institute of Local Government Studies).

Local Government Training Board (1984), *Why Local Government?*

Local Government Training Board (1985), *The Management Challenge for Local Government* (Discussion paper prepared with the Institute of Local Government Studies).

Macklin, David (1985), 'The policy debate', *Local Government Policy Making* (Spring, 1983).

Market Opinion and Research International (1985), *Residents Attitudes to Needs and Services* (Research study conducted for the London Borough of Richmond).

Maud, Sir John, Chairman, the Committee on the Management of Local Government (1967), *Volume 1: Report* (London: HMSO).

Meikle, John (1984), 'Changing the role of a district council', *Local Government Policy Making*, (November 1984).

Mobbs, Tim (1982), 'Chester-le-Street: managing with fewer managers', *Local Government Policy Making* (Spring, 1982).

Mobbs, Tim (1985), *Public Opinion and Local Democracy: Beliefs and Practices in County Cleveland* (Birmingham: The Institute of Local Government Studies).

National Consumer Council (1979), *The Consumer and the State* (London).

National Consumer Council (1983), *Measuring the Performance of Local Authorities in England and Wales – Some Consumer Principles* (A working paper).

National Council of Voluntary Organisations (1984), *Client Rights* (London: Bedford Square Press).

Neilson, Alan (1984), 'Corporate approaches and community control', *Local Government Policy Making* (July, 1984).

Nott, Steve (1982), 'Unemployment alleviation at Shotton', *Local Government Policy Making* (Summer, 1982).

Ouseley, Herman (1984), 'Local authority race initiatives', in Martin Boddy and Colin Fudge, *Local Socialism* (London: Macmillan).

Paine, Roger (1985), *Innovation in Management Practice* (A paper prepared for a Local Government Training Board seminar).

Peters, Thomas, J., and Waterman, Robert H. Jr, (1980), *In Search of Excellence* (New York, Harper & Row).

Pond, Chris (n.d.), *Low Pay: What Can Local Authorities Do?* (London: Low Pay Unit).

Rein, Martin (1976), *Social Science and Public Policy* (Harmondsworth: Penguin).

Richardson, Maureen (1985), 'Can surgeries work?', *Local Government Policy Making* (March, 1985).

Shute, Allison (1983), 'Low cost innovation in the Devon library services', *Local Government Policy Making* (Spring, 1983).

Simey, Margaret (1985), *Government by Consent* (London: Bedford Square).

SIPU (Statens Institut for Personaletveckling) (1984), *The Challenge Is On* (Salna: Sweden).

Smith, Jeff (1985), 'Clients, users, consumers and members', *Local Government Policy Making* (March, 1985).

Smith, Jerry (1985), *Public Involvement in Local Government* (London: Community Projects Foundation).

Society of Local Authority Chief Executives (1983), *The Future: Some Emerging Issues*.

Stevens, Richard (1982), *Building Better Links* (Halton District Council).

Stewart, John (1982), 'Guidelines for policy derivation', in Steve Leach and John Stewart, *Approaches in Public Policy* (London: Allen & Unwin).

Stewart, John (1983), *Local Government: The Conditions of Local Choice* (London: Allen & Unwin).

Thamesdown Borough Council (1984), *A New Vision for Thamesdown*.

Turton, Ron, (1984), *Looking Out To The Customer* (Paper prepared in LGTB Seminar).

Vickers, Sir Geoffrey (1972), *Freedom in a Rocking Boat* (Harmondsworth: Penguin).

Warwickshire County Council (1982), *Public Relations and Warwickshire County Council*.

Webster, Barbara (1983) 'Women's committees', *Local Government Policy Making* (November 1983).

Webster, Barbara, Lambeth, Christine, and Penny, Julia (n.d.), *Impact of Local Authority Services on the Inner City* (Birmingham: Institute of Local Government Studies).

Wedgwood-Oppenheim, Felix, and Baddeley, Simon (1983), 'The implications for local authorities of cable systems', *Local Government Studies* (July/August 1983).

Whiting, Tony (1983), 'When plain English became the talk of all Bradford', *Local Government Chronicle* (14 August, 1985).

Wolverhampton Borough Council (1985), *The Social Condition of Young People in Wolverhampton in 1984*.

Wychavon District Council (1985), *Wychavon: The First Ten Years*.

Young, Ken, (1982), 'Changing social services in East Sussex', *Local Government Studies* (March–April, 1982).

Young, Ken, (1984a), *The Space Between Words: Local Authorities and the Concept of Equal Opportunities*, Policy Studies Institute Working Paper.

Young, Ken, (1984b), 'Local authority operations in multi-racial areas', *Local Government Studies*, (September–October, 1984).

Young, Ken, and Kramer, J. (1978), *Strategy and Conflict in Metropolitan Housing* (London: Heinemann).

# Index